W9-DAX-085

The Bonner

media relations

Communications Series

HumberCollege
3199 Lakeshore Blvd West
Toronto, ON M8V 1K8
DISCARD

/ G C Z C /

The Bonner

media relations

Communications Series

allan bonner

Briston House
an imprint of Boheme Press

Humber College Library

Copyright © 2003 by Allan Bonner

All rights reserved. No part of this publication may be reproduced or transmitted in any form or by any means, electronic or mechanical, including photocopying or any information storage and retrieval system without a licence from Access Copyright, 1 Yonge Street, Suite 1900, Toronto, Ontario, Canada, M5E 1E5

National Library of Canada Cataloguing
in Publication Data

Bonner, Allan
Media relations / Allan Bonner

(The Bonner communication series)
Includes bibliographical references.

ISBN 1-894921-00-3

1. Public relations. 2. Mass media and business.
I. Title. II. Series: Bonner, Allan. Bonner communication series.

HD59.B65 2003   659.2   C2003-902564-0

SOCKO® is a registered trademark of Allan Bonner Communications
Management Inc.

Boheme Press gratefully acknowledges the Canada Council for the Arts
for its support of our publishing program.

Briston House, an imprint of Boheme Press
6 Lamont Creek Drive
Wasaga Beach, Ontario, L0L 2P0

For Lorna, Michael and Christian

— Table of Contents —

Foreword

My media relations experience began in the media. I was the recipient of news releases, pitches and complaints on a daily basis for 14 years. I found that many people who called me hadn't thought past the phrase "I think I have a good story for you" when they wanted me to cover something. They also hadn't thought past "that's not news" when they wanted me to kill a story.

I also found that few newsmakers had a clear, powerful message to deliver. Most sounded guilty of something. It was years before I realized that many people are just nervous of the media. That's when I decided there was room in the marketplace for a course on media relations and media training.

I left the media to join a big city mayor as Executive Assistant. He was always in the news. You may have heard of him — Mel Lastman — one of the longest serving mayors in North America. There's no secret to his success. He got up every day, bound, determined and even possessed to make news. He also made it his business to understand how radio stations, newspapers and TV stations work. I moved on from Mayor Lastman a few years later, but continue to watch his determination from afar.

Another experience which has shaped this book is conducting media relations and media training courses on five continents for some of the toughest clients in the world. When I make speeches I often ask for a show of hands to tell me who's been in a newsroom in the previous month. Then I ask who has visited a newsroom in the previous quarter or even in the last six months. I often find Public Affairs practitioners who have rarely been in newsrooms.

My goal here is to share with you what I've learned during a quarter of a century of work on both sides of the media divide. Many of the problems people have with the news media stem from a lack of knowledge about its role, its interests and motives and its workings.

This book is designed to be a handy reference for those who feel threatened by the attention of the news media, or those who feel they have a story to tell but are being ignored. It contains detailed, step-by-step advice on how to prepare for media encounters, from an unexpected "ambush" interview to a full-scale news conference and then how to follow through and maintain good media relations.

It actually began as a series of lectures to about 1,000 senior military officers across Canada. They were having a tough time getting their story told around the end of the Cold War and I was hired to give them some tools that would work. Then clients in oil and chemicals asked for tough simulations after the Valdez and Bhopal incidents and those assignments honed my knowledge as well.

Work with a great series of clients from the Government of Hong Kong to the UN in New York and from the World Trade Organization in Geneva to the NAFTA negotiating team in Canada allowed me to test my theories out in real time, real life and under real heat.

The book starts by helping you assess your own news value and leads you through the preparation you must undertake before you go anywhere near a reporter. Both the preparation and your actual encounters will be guided by my SOCKO system for key messages.

As your media needs grow, you will find ever more detailed content available — even down to the trash cans needed (but often forgotten) when setting up a temporary public affairs or media work room. Interspersed throughout are templates you can use to organize and keep track of your media relations.

I'm indebted to many people. Chief among them are my two boys, Michael and Christian, and my wife, Lorna Jackson. They endured my travel schedule for many years and have also heard me rehearse many a speech before delivery and pointed out errors and omissions. Michael has helped with semantics, of which he is a master. Christian added value to some concepts of reputation management. I was trying to show a client that there may be some benefit to a bad reputation and used the Rolling Stones as an example. Christian is an expert on them. Lorna, being a thoughtful interviewer and newscaster herself, has been a great seat mate while watching the news (while I critique it) most nights for 21 years.

Hal Jones, my senior consultant and trainer at The Centre for Training in Risk and Crisis Management, went over early drafts of this book and added structure and consistency. He's a great trainer, exemplary journalist, but the thing I'm most proud of is that, after working with me on many contentious media relations cases over seven years, we still get along.

Max Maccari at Boheme Press is a smart, young entrepreneur who saw the potential of The Bonner Communications Series. Major General Richard Rohmer has been a friend for over 25 years. He provided legal and other valuable business advice. Graphic artist, Patricia Cipolla, designed the cover and the text pages you see before you.

The errors and omissions are mine, but thanks to all who helped.

Introduction

In a span of little more than 50 years, what we now know as "the media" has grown to become one of the most significant social factors in our daily lives. It informs us, it entertains us and — whether we like it or not — it helps shape our thoughts and opinions.

It is this characteristic that makes it important for companies, organizations, institutions and some individuals to analyze their particular situations so they can decide if they need to develop a media strategy. A strategy may consist of no more than trying to avoid the media. That's not very imaginative — it may even be unrealistic — but any strategy is better than no strategy.

It is important to remember that "media" is collective: it includes all types of communication, technology and people. A weekly newspaper in a small, rural community is just as much part of the media as a national television network. The young and often inexperienced reporters who work for the former may appear to have very little in common with the photogenic anchors and correspondents of the latter. But they're all interested in a big story. And quite often what starts out as an interesting but unremarkable local story can very quickly turn out to be part of a much larger story on a national or international network.

Trade publications and programs, community cable television, shopping mall flyers and Internet sites and services are also part of the media. So are billboards, direct mail, skywriting planes and the Goodyear Blimp. They are all media of communication and all can have some impact on the way a company, organization or person is seen by others. But for all practical purposes, it is the news media and particularly the large, well-established news organizations that have the power to change the attitudes and opinions of whole communities. This is the sector of the media — the news sector — on which we will focus.

The fact that you are reading this indicates you already have an interest in knowing more about the media and how to deal with news organizations and their reporters. You may be concerned about a sensitive issue or event that is imminent or possible; it could be you just feel there is something you need to tell a larger audience; or it could be that your company or organization has decided it wants to augment the services of a dedicated public affairs department or person.

Whatever your situation, what follows will not only help you establish an over-arching communications plan, but will provide you with a wealth of practical and detailed instructions on what to do and how to do it — from writing a press release to organizing a news conference and appearing in front of the TV cameras.

It is comprehensive and easy to understand. Most of all, it is effective because it incorporates the SOCKO management system that Allan Bonner Communications Management Inc. has used while training more than 15,000 high risk and high profile clients all over the world. SOCKOs are Strategic Overriding Communications and Knowledge Objectives. As you will see later, SOCKOs provide a framework for developing and delivering messages that will help you achieve your communication goals.

Chapter 1   The Media and You

Like it or not, it's almost impossible to cut yourself off from today's news media. Step into an elevator in any office tower and you are likely to find your eyes drawn to a television monitor with a stream of numbers and stock symbols scrolling through. Restaurants, bars, waiting rooms, lobbies and even airlines have televisions tuned to 24-hour news channels or sports events (or both).

We are bombarded by news, information and data day and night. Sometimes we are interested enough to absorb parts of it. Most of the time it passes over or through us without having much impact.

But when something really interests us — be it stock prices, entertainment news, sports or human tragedy — we are influenced to some extent by the media. It is this influence that politicians, governments, corporations, entertainers and celebrities try so hard to harness.

So can you.

What is News?

Occasionally the world experiences something so dramatic or overwhelmingly important that it grabs everybody's attention. We have no doubts — THIS IS NEWS!

On an average day, however, it's far more likely that the items included in a news broadcast or newspaper will have a much more limited appeal. We wonder — and sometimes we write letters to the editor to complain — why anyone would want to PRINT SUCH DRIVEL!

Soon after World War II the US government established an official panel on Freedom of the Press which took it upon itself to try to define this nebulous thing we call "news." According to the panel, news should be a full, comprehensive and intelligent account of the day's events. News should identify fact as fact and opinion as opinion, provide full access to the day's intelligence and reflect the constituent groups in society. Now these are lofty ideals and we shouldn't be too surprised when they are not lived up to all the time.

I like the definition of news provided by the late Phil Graham of the Washington Post. He called news "The first rough draft of history." It may be important, have an impact on people and make a difference but it is being drafted on the run and so comes to us complete with errors, omissions, warts and foibles. Journalists watch the world rushing by at breakneck speed — and then present us with a snapshot of the day's events and happenings. When you look at journalists' work in that context, they don't do too badly.

Here's another definition I like. An old Australian editor once said that "news is anything that causes people to exclaim, Oh . . . !"

I'm not sure that it is possible to define news in a way that will satisfy everybody, any more than news organizations can be sure that all their readers, viewers or subscribers will approve of their selection of news items.

This may seem too vague and unsatisfying but bear in mind it is this vagueness that encourages so much diversity in the news media and allows more opportunities for ordinary people to tell their stories to their neighbours and, sometimes, to the world.

Your News Value

What we think of ourselves isn't the same as what others think of us. It's the same with companies, organizations and institutions.

Even insiders can have different views of an organization. Managers and employees are often at odds. Now broaden the frame of the picture to include customers, shareholders, competitors, suppliers, regulators, plant neighbours, financial analysts, fired employees and their dependents.

At any given time there may be several different assessments of the organization ranging from "wonderful" to "awful." Often these views balance out. Occasionally one becomes more noticeable than the other. If it's a positive view, everyone's happy and the organization prospers. But if it's negative, heads may roll and the organization may lose stature and money.

Because the news media appears to be so preoccupied with the bad stuff, most people are wary of it. Indeed, news organizations are often accused of ignoring the good to concentrate on the bad, even if the bad makes up a very small part of the whole.

Well, yes. Who, after all, is going to rush out and buy a newspaper or tune into a radio or TV program to learn that everything worked the way it should that day? Reporters and news outlets focus on things that break down, crash or fail through accident or design — because that is what people are interested in. It sells newspapers and swells audiences.

However, interspersed with all the bad stuff there's also a range of other material. Some of this material is good, some contentious and some of interest only to certain people. This is the "news" area that provides most of the public relations opportunities for people and organizations to tell others about their goals, their products or their beliefs. Unfortunately it also contains pitfalls for the unwary.

A company may be delighted to attract the attention of a major news outlet because it uses a revolutionary production technique only to find the story that appears is about the preponderance of women on the shop floor and the preponderance of men in the board room. Could this have been prevented?

There are no guarantees that organizations and people will always get positive news coverage. Even Mother Theresa had some critics. But it is possible to influence the balance of coverage by:

> Analyzing your situation: identifying weak spots as well as the strong
> Arming yourself with plenty of positive information
> Being prepared to answer difficult questions as well as easy ones
> Knowing something about the news people you are talking to

Your Situation

Draw up a balance sheet of your strong points and weak points. Be honest. If your's is a small company with private homes and a school nearby, put yourself in the shoes of a neighbour or parent and see if you'd have any concerns about your operations.

You can get a good idea of the concerns the community may have about you by reviewing the regulatory and licensing requirements of your operations.

If your enterprise is part of a sector that has made news elsewhere because something went wrong, you may be asked what you are doing to change your operations to ensure the same thing doesn't happen in your locality.

Look at your strong points. Do they contain something that would interest others, either the community at large or others like you? How would you go about telling them?

Being Positive

Most organizations and enterprises these days have mission statements and/or vision statements. But our experience is that few people have the ability to state simply and clearly what they or their organizations do. It seems so obvious to them they never consider that it may not be so obvious to others. This results in a lot of lost opportunities to make a positive impression.

The solution is to arm yourself with as many positive statements as possible about yourself and your activities and watch for opportunities to use them.

Questions

We ask questions of others to elicit information, imply criticism, display our knowledge or, sometimes, just to keep the conversation going. But we seldom analyze why others are asking questions of us. If we find the questions difficult, we can get upset; if irrelevant we can be dismissive. But in both instances we are missing opportunities to communicate something positive about ourselves or our organizations.

News Media

Study the news organizations you are most likely to come into contact with — or want to contact. Are they local, national, trade or professionally oriented?

In the days of the Soviet Union, you would hear the people of Eastern Europe joke "Visit Russia — before it visits you!" If you think you may be visited by a news organization in the future, visit it first.

Find out what kind of news the organization is interested in and what it is about you that may interest its reporters. Better still, try to get some background information about you and/or your organization into the hands of a reporter or editor who may have an interest in the same field even if not the same specific subject matter.

Media Relations

The most challenging aspect for any organization's public affairs department is the media relations function. These titles for the Department in which communicators work have changed over time and are different in different organizations. Just as the Personnel Department became the Human Resources Department, the term Public Relations has changed into Public Affairs or Communication. Public Affairs implies that the organization is involved in issues of interest and importance to members of the public. Communication implies a variety of technical activities designed to move information from person to person and place to place. This might include advertising and direct mail. Some of my clients still use the old fashioned sounding term "press office." I prefer Public Affairs.

There's a similar debate about the terms stakeholder and public. Some Public Affairs professionals refer to their "publics." This means customers, neighbours, suppliers, workers and others. Stakeholders can mean any who have a legitimate stake in what the organization is doing, including bankers, regulators, legislators and others. I've always felt that "public" implies that the issue is of known, public importance, and this would include neighbours, media, customers and politicians. It may also include regulators. Stakeholders seems to imply a more private relationship, including bankers, workers and perhaps regulators. But you can easily see how issues can move from being private to public, depending on the type of organization. For many practical purposes, these terms are interchangeable.

Effective media relations can save an organization's reputation and commercial viability when something goes tragically wrong, as in the Tylenol poisoning case (Fall of 1982), the Coors appearance on 60 Minutes during a reputation management issue (April 1982), and Lee Iacocca's forthright dealing with an odometer spinning controversy at Chrysler (July 1987). Despite serious and often true charges against him, President Bill Clinton seemed to be able to repeatedly use the media to salvage his reputation.

Poor media relations can have the opposite effect as in the nuclear accident at Three Mile Island, Pennsylvania which irrevocably tarnished the nuclear industry's safety image; the chemical release in Bhopal, India (December 1984) and the Exxon Valdez oil spill (March 1989). More recently, the negative news stories about accounting procedures and their effect on stock prices seem to get worse as a result of poor communication.

Although all of the above examples cite large organizations with large professional public affairs and media relations departments, size isn't a factor. Attitude is.

Some organizations feel they can be silent when information is sought by reporters and will attempt to "tough it out." Experience shows this is not advisable since it merely creates an information vacuum into which others will step, and those others usually have their own agendas. Thus, it is important for an organization to attempt to be the most accurate and reliable source of information about its own activities. Spokespeople must be available and the organization must be seen to be cooperative and active.

The power of the news media is often misunderstood. While the news media has its failings, there's no doubt that it helps shape and direct public opinion. Much of its power depends on its ability to disseminate information extremely quickly. It takes very few key people to decide that an event is big enough to be broadcast live around the world, where it will be watched by billions of people. That's power.

At the same time we know the media can be ineffective in separating fact from perception and correcting misconceptions or inaccuracies. George Bernard Shaw once dismissed the media for being "unable, seemingly, to discriminate between a bicycle accident and the collapse of civilization."

While reporters, line up editors and producers may often overreact or have misplaced priorities, you dismiss or ignore the media at your peril. Organizations must actively participate in the information flow.

This is particularly true when reporters are interested in a potentially negative story. If there is a problem, acknowledge it — then enumerate the actions being taken to correct the situation. This same information should be provided to stakeholders. All communications and actions should be taken with the focus on the long term interests of the stakeholders. Each direct contact with the stakeholders or contact with the media should be viewed as an opportunity to transmit the organization's message and build rapport. The questions and needs of all stakeholders including the media should be anticipated and met in a timely fashion.

During these times, the news media will ask for, consume, collate and disseminate more information at a higher rate of speed and more widely than public affairs managers can anticipate. It is important that the company address this insatiable appetite with the attitude that the media and the public they serve have proper reasons for inquiring about the status of an event.

No purpose will be served by questioning why the media require as much information as they do as quickly as they do.

It will be important to use charts, graphs, status boards, cork boards or other means in media briefing or news conference rooms to keep reporters up-to-date on as many facts as possible. Assemble those facts by asking the traditional journalistic questions WHO, WHEN, WHAT, WHERE, WHY and HOW.

Some of these questions present special legal predicaments. There should be no speculation on the exact cause of an event or incident unless it is completely obvious. The same is true of liability and responsibility. In most cases these issues should not be addressed by anyone other than senior management. But senior management should also protect the organization's credibility in cases where the answers to these questions are completely obvious. Beware of being too optimistic too early. You may not get back to normal or clean up the mess as quickly as you predict.

Formal media monitoring is available from several companies and is the only effective way to know exactly what news reports said about you. Coverage of your statements and those by politicians and others about you should be monitored and analyzed by an independent team on a regular basis to allow for a proper response strategy. This monitoring and/or analysis should include communication from other significant stakeholders including telephone calls from customers, the public, suppliers and bankers.

Irrespective of the level and frequency of contact with the news media, organizations and individuals need to be clear in their own minds of what they want to say before they start talking to reporters.

They need SOCKOS.

Chapter 2   Arm Yourself

SOCKO: A Definition

(so kó) n. acronym for Strategic Overriding Communications and Knowledge Objective. 1. A short, positive, sharp, memorable, honed, polished, true, unassailable statement. 2. A "media-genic" clip or quotation on radio, TV, or in newspaper stories. 3. A 20-second or less, quotable quote, with impact, often showing caring, knowledge and/or action. 4. A rough equivalent to a headline, cutline or lead, best delivered after full rehearsal at least 3 times, e.g. "I have nothing to offer but blood, toil, tears and sweat," ". . . ask not what your country can do for you; ask what you can do for your country . . . ." "just watch me . . . ."

The Power of SOCKOs

You probably have considerable knowledge about your chosen field. Unfortunately that does not ensure you'll be able to describe your work and beliefs clearly and succinctly to the media.

We've found that most people take their daily life and activity so much for granted they just assume that others will have no difficulty in understanding their explanations. When asked by an interviewer "What do you do, why do you do it and is it important?" they look and sound uncomfortable as they struggle to put their thoughts into words.
It doesn't have to be like that.

The SOCKO system has helped people in many parts of the world to be better communicators. It has proved its value in high-profile situations with politicians, diplomats, military leaders, trade negotiators and other public officials. It's also worked with business executives, police officers, lawyers and social institutions.

The SOCKO system helps you speak more effectively because SOCKOs help you identify your objectives and then stay focused on them.

You may already have encountered, or heard of, "key messages," "aces," " press lines" or some other term used to describe a sentence or phrase containing the information you would like to be able to deliver to an audience.

While similar to SOCKOs, there is one vital difference: SOCKOs are designed to have an impact-just as the acronym suggests.

The acronym stands for Strategic Overriding Communications and Knowledge Objectives.

The SOCKO system starts with strategic thinking.

Strategic

Imagine a knock on your office door and a senior vice-president asks you to step outside and give a status report on Project X , Issue Y or File Z to a visiting VIP. You have a strategic decision to make. Do you reply, "Sorry, I'm too busy right now coping with issue C or file D" or do you step out into the hall and give that briefing?

Not surprisingly, most people would give the briefing. Many would do the same even if it were a reporter who walked up at a conference and asked for a quick interview. Few will take the time or trouble to compose themselves, think about what they want to say and then rehearse it.

The most effective way to improve oral communication is to practise out L-O-U-D, but most people have a built-in resistance to doing this, especially if someone else can hear them.

It's quite different with written communications. A briefing paper for senior management is likely to be written, reviewed and re-written several times before it's passed up the chain of command. We tend to treat written communication with much more care and reverence than oral statements — and yet these days, because of the media, oral communications are enormously important. Even when you're dealing with print reporters, you need to remember that the medium of communication is speech, not print.

Strategic thinking for the media relations function not only means serious thought about what you are going to say, but also attention to what kind of messenger you are going to be. Rehearsing out loud will catch many errors, omissions, bafflegab and just plain boring statements.

Rehearsing with a colleague, family member, public affairs specialist or outside consultant will catch more.

We find with our clients that still other obstacles to clear communication emerge when we ask them to draw their message during a practice session. This forces the speaker to make sure the message is concrete and that helps the reporter and audience "see" what's being discussed.

But the strategy doesn't stop there. We use something we call 360 degree learning that surrounds the participants and immerses the spokesperson in the message. Participants talk through their messages, draw them, hear others talk about the message and pose questions about the topic.

We find that most spokespeople have a general platitude about an issue. But very few can say how news consumers can benefit from the topic under discussion. Fewer still can give specifics on how they are going about their stated goals. It's difficult to get this specific, but we insist that spokespeople know how to answer the fifth, sixth and seventh questions asked, not just the first and second. This cannot be done without practice and strategic thinking before walking out to the cameras and microphones.

The other necessary activity is to inject humanity into the performance. Most senior executives spend their lives in front of computer screens, reading documents and talking into the telephone. But to be a convincing spokesperson is a performance art. People buy people first.

I often tell clients that what a TV audience is buying is "eyeballs." You have to look the reporter or camera in the eye if it's a double-ender or videographer and be believable. In training sessions, we insist that spokespeople not only demonstrate their knowledge of a topic and the action they are going to take, but also the caring they have for the issue.

Without expressing caring, the spokesperson is just another "talking head," wasting our time on TV. Caring comes through on radio as well, and a print reporter will judge you, in part, on whether you transmit your caring, compassion and passion about a topic.

Overriding

The average human ear connected to the average human brain takes in just 35% of what it hears. The amount remembered after one week is just 10%. It might even be less with busy reporters who are hearing lots of "spin" on any given day.

You have to make a special effort to get reporters to listen to you and understand what you're saying.

The first thing you must do is identify and gather all the various messages you intend to deliver. Write them down. Then try to visualize this mass of information you have gathered to be in the shape of an iceberg.

The most important information you want to convey is like the tip of the iceberg — only 10% of all the information you have on your subject. This is the equivalent of the reporter's lead, except it's your perspective on the issue, not the reporter's.

Imagine you are on a bus and a passenger says to you: "I notice from your briefcase that you're with X-Y-Z Corporation. Didn't I read something bad about your company recently? What's going on?"

Your questioner then pulls the signal to indicate he wants to get off at the next stop. You have 8 seconds to tell that person the most important things you know about your organization.

If your questioner decides to stay on the bus to hear more, you can reinforce your message by delivering the next most important 10% of your information, and so on.

In Hollywood, it's called your "elevator pitch." You enter an elevator and press number 20 when someone else enters and presses number 10. It turns out to be a famous producer and you have only a few seconds to pitch your movie idea before he gets off and vanishes. It had better be good. That's where the SOCKO system comes in.

The SOCKO system is similar to the way newspaper stories used to be prepared in the days before newsrooms were computerized and printing presses still used hot type.

Reporters working on a story near deadline would type their copy on short pieces of paper that would hold only a few sentences. Then the reporter would yell, "Copy!" to summon a copy boy who'd take those few sentences to the editor's desk for checking before they could be sent down to the composing room for inclusion in the newspaper.

This process continued until either the story was complete or, more likely, the clock ran out and the composing room advised that the page was "locked" and the paper had been "put to bed." Because of the danger of running out of time, reporters would put the most important facts at the top of the story. Besides, readers often stop reading before they get to the end of a story. That's the reason for the inverted pyramid structure for print stories. It would take extraordinary circumstances for the editor to "stop the presses" so that new information could be included.

SOCKOs, and the gradual and sequential release of them in order of importance is the spokesperson's equivalent of the reporter typing on deadline. The analogy continues because at any moment in your journalistic encounter, the reporter might say "thank you," and your opportunity is over. In this environment, you need brevity, clarity, simplicity and your most important messages on the tip of your tongue.

Communication

Nobody wants to read the same phrase or sentence over and over again. We'd assume the writer was too lazy to edit his or her work. But in oral communication, repetition is not only desirable but mandatory if you want your message to be clearly understood and believed.

Shakespeare was well aware of this and used repetition to good effect to assist comprehension in the primitive theatres where his plays were first performed.

The original Globe Theatre in London had only a bare stage with little or no scenery. Plays had to be staged in daylight because there was no electricity. In those days there could be two or three thousand people milling around in the "pit" at the front of the stage and in the seats, talking, laughing, arguing or fighting. Drunks, pickpockets and hookers were plentiful. Ushers and bouncers hadn't been invented.

This was the daunting atmosphere confronting actors who'd appear on the stage without the benefit of dimming house lights and raising curtains to begin the performance. Imagine all that noise and distraction. Perhaps 500 audience members had their backs to the stage and another

1000 were in mid-sentence with a seat mate. In the middle of all this, two actors walk out on stage and start talking:

Bernardo:	Who's there?
Francisco:	Nay, answer me; stand, and unfold yourself.
Bernardo:	Long live the king!
Francisco:	Bernardo?
Bernardo:	He.
Francisco:	You come most carefully upon your hour.
Bernardo:	'Tis now struck twelve, get thee to bed, Francisco.
Francisco:	For this relief much thanks; 'tis bitter cold, And I am sick at heart.
Bernardo:	Have you had quiet guard?
Francisco:	Not a mouse stirring.
Bernardo:	Well, good night. If you do meet Horatio and Marcellus, The rivals of my watch, bid them make haste.
	[Enter Horatio and Marcellus]
Francisco:	I think I hear them. Stand, ho! Who is there?
Horatio:	Friends to this ground.
Marcellus:	And liegemen to the Dane.
Francisco:	Give you good night.
Marcellus:	O, farewell, honest soldier. Who hath reliev'd you?
Francisco:	Bernardo hath my place. Give you good night.
	[Exit Francisco]
Marcellus:	Holla! Bernardo!
Bernardo:	Say-what, is Horatio there?
Horatio:	A piece of him.
Bernardo:	Welcome, Horatio; welcome, good Marcellus.
Marcellus:	What, has this thing appear'd again to-night?

Shakespeare was no fool. He recognized the limitations of the venues for his plays and actors. He knew that most of his words would go literally and figuratively over the heads of his audience. He knew his audience had distractions. So he used a very simple technique: repetition. He had his actors tell us over and over again that it's night.

It takes me about eight minutes to read the Act I of Hamlet out loud. In that short time, the actors mention directly that it is night 16 times ("Give you good night!) and indirectly 19 times (cold, sick at heart, quiet guard etc). At my rate or reading, the time of day is mentioned every 14 seconds. No matter how distracted you are, you are going to know the time of day.

This is a formula that worked well for Shakespeare and he repeated it often. He was also fond of using triptychs: "friends, Romans, country-men" or "thus, I die, die, die." Imagine yourself on that 10-foot-high stage almost surrounded by three rows of audience members. Deliver one of the triptych's words to the front, another to your left and the last to your right. As Shakespeare intended, and you are including everyone.

Simplicity, brevity, clarity and repetition. If it was good enough for Shakespeare, it's good enough for you.

Because the ear is such an imperfect instrument there isn't much point in exposing it to extremely complicated words and messages. The average university student has difficulty comprehending a sentence longer than 18 words. When speaking to reporters, keep it short and keep it simple.

We know that visual aids help a presentation, whether on paper or in the boardroom. Graphs, maps, charts and diagrams can increase retention by as much as 50%. But did you know that studies show the same is true for oral communication? The same senior executives who wouldn't dream of going into the boardroom without visual aids think nothing of going into a media encounter without anecdotes, stories and examples — the verbal equivalent of visual aids.

The key is to tell a story and paint a word picture. Don't be afraid to use trigger phrases such as "picture this . . . imagine the following . . . our visions is . . . what we see is . . . what I'd like you to see is . . . ." These phrases will trigger verbal, visual aids as you speak. Think visually and increase the power of your media sound bites, clips or actualities.

Knowledge

Any time you come into contact with the media, they will expect you to have basic factual information about your company or organization at your fingertips. The number of employees in the building at any given time, percentages of women and visible minorities, number of vehicles, annual sales, the number of annual fire drills — all of these provide a picture of the organization.

Make sure you have these basic facts ready today. Tomorrow may be too late.

Your familiarity with your organization and your capability in using this information to describe activities or support a course of action or belief can have a major impact on those listening and what they think of you and the organization.

Objective

This isn't the same kind of objectivity some people say they want from journalists. There's no such thing. No editor would send a journalist out to cover child abuse and instruct him to get both sides of the story. Few readers would want such "objectivity." What you can hope for is fairness, balance, accuracy or completeness.

So, the kind of "objective" meant by the final "O" in SOCKO refers to the measurable, quantifiable, human, behavioural or tangible result that you want to achieve through your communication with reporters.

When you are dealing with reporters, those objectives need to be headlines, leads, quotes, pictures, cut-lines, sub-heads, side-bars, call-outs, b-roll and clips. These are the elements that reporters use to convey a story:

Headlines	The big print that announces the story and makes you read on.
Subhead	An important aspect to the story that may catch readers' eyes.

Lead	The first sentence or paragraph of a story which gets to the point quickly.
Quote	Your words in print, in quotation marks.
Pictures	The visual element in print or television.
Cut-lines	The caption for a picture in a newspaper — the words right under the picture.
Side-bar	A parenthetical story-background or context.
Call-out	A few words of a print story isolated and enlarged to add punch or graphic appeal to the printed page.
B-roll	Descriptive video footage used to illustrate a TV news item, often used in editing quotes and other elements together.
Clips	Quotes from you, also known as actuality, sound ups or sound bites (parts of interviews).

Quotes and clips are the elements over which you have the most influence because they are your words (or SOCKOs). Remember that the average length of a clip on a television or radio news in controversial situations is about 8 seconds. Public broadcasters and documentary producers may use longer clips; tabloid television and rock radio stations may use shorter clips.

As you frame your messages you must think in media-genic terms and you must be brief. If you are not thinking in terms of quotes, headlines etc. your message will not be in a format that is useful to the reporter. The reporter is going to have to convert your message into a news format, and there's no guarantee your message will survive intact. You must deliver your message in a format the audience can recognize and make use of. The less it is edited or modified, the better.

The more you can visualize your objectives in real, human, behavioural terms, the more you will achieve them. You want the reporter to use your clip and write the story from your perspective. You want the reporter's audience at home to see the world the way you do and act in a certain way. You must define these behaviours very clearly to achieve your objective. Now is the time to write out exactly what you want the listeners, readers and viewers of your news story to do and visualize them doing it.

Now that we have defined a SOCKO and given it form — an iceberg

— it's time to give it some substance, to put some meat on its bones so that you can begin to see how the SOCKO system can work for you and your organization.

Think about your three most important issues. These are the issues you really want reporters and the world to know about you, your corporation, its policies, organization, hopes, goals and aspirations. They could also be the issues the world is dying to find out about you, whether you like it or not!

These topics or issues take the form of brief headings. Typical issues might be funding, compliance, investor confidence, ethics, health, safety and so on. This is a perfect opportunity for you to take stock of what is really important to you and your organization.

The format to follow is: ISSUE-SOCKO-DISCUSSION. The issues are designed to do no more than trigger stimulus response in your message delivery. They need to be general enough so that your SOCKO can address any number of specific questions concerning that issue.

It doesn't matter if a question dealing with costs is phrased to ask if it is too expensive, or how you are going to pay for it, or even who will pay for it? Your cost ISSUE should contain a generic SOCKO that can respond to many of the questions that deal with cost. One good SOCKO happens to address many questions that might be asked. That doesn't mean you only need one SOCKO — you need many. But it does mean that you get multiple use out of the SOCKOs you have. Many large organizations rely heavily on a "questions and answer" format but I prefer SOCKOs. There are an endless number of ways to phrase questions and thus an endless set of answers to prepare. I'd rather make multiple use SOCKOs than start a Q & A project that, by definition, never ends.

A great SOCKO just may be the answer to 50 questions you might be asked. But, a Q & A sheet has only one answer per question. With SOCKOs, you use versions of them over and over again. I say versions because you don't want to sound scripted.

Qs & As are like a "round" in music. The most famous round is probably "row, row, row your boat." Each person says the same thing, at the same time in the round, with the same notes, over and over again. It both sounds and is repetitive. A Bach "fugue," however, has several variations. The composer has some choice of when to come in, on what note and with what sequence of notes. It still has structure, but a fugue generates and sustains more interest than a round.

The kind of repetition you want is the kind Shakespeare used-emphatic, clear and powerful repetition, not redundant repetition.

Once you've identified your ISSUE, you should decide which is the most important 10% of the information about which you want to tell the world. This is your SOCKO.

After that you can add four or five supporting discussion points that you can use to expand your answer when you respond to follow up questions. This way you make sure you have enough material to present and defend your case, no matter how rigorous the interrogation. It might help if you also think of your SOCKOs as the raw material of news.

Framing

Framing is important because it places your message in context. If you don't care enough about your message to place it in context, don't be surprised if reporters choose the context for you. When people in the public eye complain that they have been misquoted in the media, what they usually means is that their words have been taken out of context.

So set your own frame.

Imagine anchoring yourself in the graphic frame in this book and be sure not to let anyone pull you out. You aren't in total control here because the people receiving your message may have their own frames, or modify yours based on their personal experiences. You may say the glass is half full while they are convinced it is half empty.

Social scientists tell us that the person or group that sets a valid frame first on any given issue has a tremendous advantage over those who try to do so later. It is very hard to un-frame a message, un-spin it, put the genie back in the bottle or the toothpaste back in the tube. As one academic put it: "It's hard to un-scare people."

Parents know that going, "Boo!" is the easy part, but consoling a scared toddler can be tough.

So make you message powerful and clear and get it out early and often and you will always be ahead of your adversaries.

Your message can also be a "flag" or signal to the audience that you are worth listening to and your issue is worth paying attention to. The signal potential of a message involves a subliminal communication that you and your message are more important than all the other things competing for the attention of the recipient that day. Considering the "all news" formats of many radio and TV stations and the thousands of other distractions in a day, you have to work hard for a share of the news consumers' minds. SOCKOs will help you do just that.

Messages have to compete to survive. Your message may signal that this issue or event is a harbinger of things to come. It's got "legs" and will be around for a while. That can be good or bad, depending on the issue and the side you're on, but that's how the system works.

Amplification helps explain how some minor issues can capture media attention, and how an issue moves between and among various players in society, such as lawyers, clergy, activists and others. The issue changes during this journey and your management of the issue must change also. I liken the journey that an issue takes through the various players in society to the path through a pinball machine that the steel ball takes. You have to guide the ball, play the flippers and be careful to not tilt the machine.

Amplification is also the reason that some messages "override" other messages. Terms such as "ecologist," "fisherman" or "aboriginal" had more resonance or amplification power than "oil company" did after the Exxon oil spill in Valdez, Alaska.

So, some words "trump" other words. Similarly, most images trump most words and some images trump other images. This means that the images of the endangered bald eagle, the dead otter and the oiled bird trumped all other concepts, messages and images in the Valdez oil spill. Most of the technically competent engineers, scientists and others who worked for Exxon thought that the plain, unvarnished facts of the matter would win the day. Even though the facts were on their side, simple recitation of those facts didn't stand a chance against those images.

You need to construct your words and images to fight and win the battle against other powerful and competing messages.

Another way of looking at amplification is to illustrate your position, idea or initiative by linking it to something that is already well known. I worked with the spokesperson of a prestigious Washington think tank recently and was a little surprised how easily he adopted this approach. It turned out he already kept an eye on popular songs and movies so that he could turn a memorable phrase in his media clips and quotes. That may sound superficial, but if it works and gets your perspective out, it's worth a try.

Now is the time to use these principles and methods outlined above. We're convinced that it's not only possible, but also necessary for organizations to identify the thirty or so topics about which they may have to speak and work through what they're going to say on these topics. This work needs to be done now, well in advance of media scrutiny.

Even a good news opportunity is no time for a company or organization to begin the process of deciding how it can best describe its activities, its goals, hopes or aspirations. Doing so during a crisis or unforeseen circumstance is foolhardy.

Let's say a building blows up. As a spokesperson you'll be asked: "Was anybody killed? How did they die? How badly are people injured? Are you insured? Are you liable for third party damages? How did it happen? What was the cause? How bad is the damage? Can the building be fixed? When do you expect to reopen for business?" On the assumption that you are not a physician, lawyer, police officer, insurance adjuster and anti-terrorist specialist all rolled into one, the answer to all those questions must be: "I don't know."

But you can't walk out to face the cameras and microphones and say, "Here's a list of all the thing I don't know." You have to say something. So, you talk about strategies, attitudes, behaviour, goals, hopes, aspirations, capabilities and training — but only if you and your organization have had the foresight and taken the trouble to prepare these SOCKOs in advance.

Newsmakers prepare a series of basic SOCKOs using everyday language as part of an effective and successful communications strategy. A manual containing SOCKOs covering a variety of topics and issues should be compiled and updated as necessary.

SOCKOs are essential to have in media encounters, whether over the telephone, in person, on camera, with a print reporter or on background with an editorial board.

Now that you have your SOCKOs in hand and some ideas of how they can be deployed in the service of your organization or company, it's time to go to work.

Most stations and networks have their own ideas of what is practical and aesthetically pleasing. Here, the London studios of CNBC Europe involve a formal setting with lots of desk and space between me and the host.

Chapter 3 Get Ready

Before you rush out to schmooze with reporters and hope to influence the media you better be sure in your own mind of what you are doing, why you are doing it and what you hope to achieve. Celebrities can joke they don't care what the media says about them so long as their names are spelled correctly, but most of us can't take that chance.

You need to prepare. You need a plan.

Preparation

A good way to start is by drawing up a short list of achievable media goals that will support your organization's overall objectives. A company that makes reciprocating widgets for a niche market has a better chance of being known as a leader in its own field than as a national economic symbol.

In this case, the list of goals could be:

1.   A cover or other major story about the company in the quarterly Widget Report.

2.   A letter to the editor of the local paper on some community issue involving employees (i.e. The United Way, Adult Education etc.).

3.   An offer to assist the national Science TV channel when it gets around to producing a program on "Widgets through the Ages."

At the same time, you will have to draft a policy for your organization as to who is responsible for implementing the media relations policy and communicating with reporters and editors.

Among other things this will:

> Set out how the organization will respond to media inquires, whether those inquiries are welcome or not
> Ensure that all media inquires are directed to the appropriate people (i.e. Media Relations Specialist, Public Affairs Department or Plant Manager)
> Identify those authorized to speak to the media on behalf of the organization

This policy should be distributed throughout the organization, with details such as names and phone numbers being updated regularly. How you handle incoming media calls will depend on several factors including:

> the size of your organization
> the number of office locations/plants and their distance from head office
> the proximity of the journalist because distance and time zones can dictate whether the interaction is in person or by phone, and which location handles the inquiry
> whether you have a Public Affairs Department or person
> the skills and interest of senior management
> the topic, since technical issues may have to be handled by engineers or other knowledgeable spokespeople

The very fact that you have a communications policy will make it clear to those involved in your organization or company that this is a matter of considerable importance.

Furthermore, drafting and writing such a policy will help you think through these issues and will cause senior management and the Board to think through them. Its provisions will be those you have considered carefully and have adapted and adopted because they fit your particular circumstances.

Such a policy could look something like this:

Title: Media Management and External Communications

1.0 APPLICABILITY

This policy is for XYZ Corporation and all employees of XYZ Corporation.

2.0 PURPOSE

The purpose of this document is to outline the steps to be followed when managing external communications under pressure or at any time that an employee of XYZ Corporation is communicating on behalf of XYZ Corporation in a public forum.

Any one of three different circumstances may be included:

> Communications with the media during a crisis (Section 4.0)
> Communications with the media during a "good" news event i.e. product launch, investment, public service event (Section 5.0)
> When an XYZ Corporation employee fulfills a "public" or "industry" or "stakeholder" speaking engagement (Section 6.0)

3.0 GENERAL

3.1 XYZ Corporation has issued a number of Strategic Overriding Communications Knowledge Objective (SOCKO) statements, which represent the company's key message on issues and/or topics. Spokespeople must confine their communication to these issues — "when in doubt, leave it out."

3.2 Media communications and questions raised may present special legal predicaments. There should be no speculation on the exact cause of the incident unless it is completely obvious and agreed upon by the Crisis Team. The same is true for liability and responsibility. In most cases these issues should not be addressed by anyone other than Executive members. But the Executive should also protect the company's credibility in cases where answers to these questions are completely obvious.

3.3 Care should also be taken in overly optimistic statements regarding remedies or solutions to the problem.

3.4 Speaking in public during a crisis or controversy is not only a challenge for the individual, but may be a pivotal point for XYZ Corporation.

3.5 Spokesperson training is essential for all individuals who are expected to speak on behalf of the company. Such training should be held annually within the company. Refresher and issue-specific training must occur during a crisis before any spokesperson speaks on behalf of the corporation. In extreme situations, this can be a rehearsal with the Director of Communications and/or other knowledgeable executives, but is ideally done with an outsider trained to pose challenging questions.

3.6 Each direct contact with the stakeholders or contact with the media should be viewed as an opportunity to transmit the company's message or SOCKO and enhance trust and rapport. All communications and focus should be on the long-term interests of all stakeholders.

4.0 CRISIS COMMUNICATIONS

4.1 A crisis is generally defined as an unexpected and unstable incident that brings on radical or rapid change. Its causes often seem beyond the control of managers, the occurrences spontaneous and the outcome capable of producing decisive variances from the norm. Proper response can tax resources to the limit or be beyond the capability of existing resources. The eventual outcomes can be both positive and negative for the company since a crisis is a turning point for better or worse.

4.2 As it relates to XYZ Corporation, a crisis is an occurrence that has the potential for adversely affecting the reputation and/or tangible assets of the company. For the purposes of this manual, crisis is broadly defined as an incident involving the corporation that could likely:
a) Jeopardize the life or health of employees, their families, the community or consumers of products.
b) Significantly impact assets or profits.

c)   Result in conditions detrimental to the corporation's public image, customer confidence or shareholders' trust.

4.3 Crisis situations usually evoke visceral reactions that remain long after the incident has taken place and transcend the realm of traditional corporate management. Actions necessary to effectively deal with these events involve decision-making, management organization and communications beyond the typical business approach. Timelines and the organizational hierarchy are compressed. Media management may be a significant aspect of crisis management.

All inquiries from national or international media should be coordinated with Corporate Communications. The Director of Communications is the person responsible for this coordination. See the "Corporate Communications and Investor Relations" home page for key Corporate Communications contacts.

Only designated spokespeople or the Director of Communication will engage in crisis communications with the media at XYZ Corporation. If these include subject matter experts, they must confine their communication to those subject areas.

If the Executive believes that a crisis will be a prolonged event or will gain significant media attention, immediate media monitoring will be initiated through a company that provides this service. Electronic coverage as well as public statements by politicians or others should be monitored and analyzed on a regular basis to allow for a proper response strategy.

Monitoring might include calls to customers, suppliers etc to determine their perceptions of the events and communication effectiveness.

5.0 INITIATED MEDIA COMMUNICATIONS

5.1 "Good" news events such as a product launch, investment or public service events will be will be managed by the Director of Communications who will be responsible for:

a)   Identifying appropriate spokespeople and providing them with the necessary training to be effective.

b)   Arranging for external communications consulting support, where necessary.

c)   Overseeing the drafting and approval of Strategic Overriding

Communications Knowledge Objective (SOCKO) statements, which represent the company's positions on a variety of issues and activities.

6.0   PUBLIC COMMUNICATIONS

6.1 Employees who can be identified as representatives of XYZ Corporation must advise Management and seek approval before making any remarks about the Corporation in public.

6.2 Specified senior members of Management may grant approval for such requests after determining whether or not they are based on and support the Corporation's views and policies.

7.0 GENERAL PROCEDURES

7.1 The Director of Communication, or delegate, shall be responsible for managing external and internal communications of XYZ Corporation.

7.2 All media inquiries shall be referred to the Director of Communication or a specified Spokesperson for XYZ Corporation. Following an interview, the spokesperson shall inform the Director of Communication of the nature of the questions asked and answers given. XYZ Corporation will maintain the technical ability to record telephone conversations with reporters and use this capability on a case-by-case basis. Spokespeople will matter-of-factly inform journalists that they are recording the conversation in order to accurately inform other executives about the conversation.

7.3 When reporters call, gain some time to think:
> Find out whom they represent
> Find out if they are a journalist, researcher or producer
> Ask, "what is your deadline?"
> Ask "what the segment or article will be about?"

Refer to the appropriate spokesperson or to the Director of Communication or a member of the Executive if necessary.

Next steps:

> Discover what approach they are taking
> Ask what research, reports, and documents have been seen. Offer your own
> Ask what areas of discussion they would like to cover
> Find out where the interview will take place
> Ask who else will be interviewed
> Discover date of airing or publication
> Ask how long the interview will last
> Ask how detrimental it would be to refuse the interview. If so, the spokesperson must refer to the appropriate corporate SOCKOs. It may be necessary to construct new SOCKOs, and involve subject matter experts and the Director of Communication

7.4 The spokesperson will then, in consultation with the Director of Communication if necessary, determine if it is in the Corporation's best interests to participate in the interview. If so, the spokesperson must refer to the appropriate corporate SOCKOs. It may be necessary to construct new SOCKOs and involve subject matter experts and the Director of Communication. The spokesperson must then rehearse these and prepare thoroughly for the media encounter.

During the interview, the spokesperson needs to:
> Control the agenda
> Be confident through knowledge of corporate SOCKOs
> Be credible through preparation & knowledge
> Repeat the SOCKOs frequently
> Avoid repeating the interviewer's negatives but bridge to the key message

7.5 The spokesperson's job is not only to answer the questions but to communicate SOCKOs and stress the caring, knowledge and action components of the overall message.

7.6 Post-interview, the spokesperson must immediately brief the Director of Communications on the content of the encounter. The spokesperson must have a written and/or taped record of the encounter, depending on the situation.

Communications Matrix

Public affairs is a complex function. Media relations is just one set of activities, but there's also investor relations, public relations, employee relations, customer relations, advertising, direct mail, web pages, open houses and a seemingly endless list of activities. The communications matrix is one way to codify where media relations fits into the various other activities the public affairs professional needs to handle.

Large organizations and institutions with public affairs departments know the value of maintaining regular contacts with the media and others. But this is just as important for smaller entities whose staff and managers are too busy just keeping the enterprise functioning without having to worry about public relations.

What follows is a practical guide to establishing a solid foundation for media and public relations.

Public affairs and other officials must take on the responsibility of regularly communicating with the media, significant community groups and other stakeholders. The Communications Matrix (See Appendix 1, Figure 3.1) is one method of analyzing these groups, listing activities by which organizations can interact with them, measuring and attempting to quantify the desired result, budgeting and assigning responsibilities.

This is a draft, but it does illustrate some potential activities. For example, it may be in the best interests of the organizations to keep the lines of communication open with the chair of a legislative or Regulatory Committee even if there is not a current issue to warrant contact. Thus, a system of regular phone calls indicating openness and availability may be useful. This activity could occur when a relatively uncontroversial issue surfaces so that during times of controversy the Chair or other members will have previously interacted with the organization.

Government lists should be kept up to date semi-annually, as should a list of other officials with whom locations and operating companies come into contact.

Formal meetings with newspaper editorial boards can be very useful. These boards are generally composed of those responsible for the publication's editorials. They often meet with newsmakers or people with specialized knowledge. Often they are joined by reporters who would normally cover the field encompassing the topic under discussion.

If you think your organization's activities have, or may have, an impact on the community, its people, the government, its policies or the economy an editorial board may be interested in talking to the CEO, Chair or other selected representative. Call them and ask.

It is a dangerous and unacceptable circumstance to have editorial writers helping to shape the community's opinions about organizations if they have never met or been briefed by a senior official of that organization.

It is also risky to have a representative of an organization interviewed by a journalist if that journalist is interacting with the company for the first time. Thus, a system of regular contacts with reporters, editors and interviewers is essential. This interaction may be as simple as sending them a background briefing paper, a public service announcement, a pamphlet or another document semi-annually.

Only through such interactions can a company or organization become familiar with a news organization's internal workings and "pecking order." For example, "the editor" may be the person responsible for the entire news operation in one organization, but only certain types of stories in another, just editorials in another, a certain beat or something completely different.

In television news, it is important to keep track of the various "assignment editors." These are the people who consider a subject, person or organization newsworthy enough to despatch a camera crew and/or reporter to get a story. Smaller television outlets may have one or two, networks have several-responsible for national news, local news, sports, business and so on.

Once it is determined that the company or organization should interact with the media and others, the implementation of this Communications Matrix will be an ongoing task. New people or groups may be regularly added to the matrix since media people are highly mobile.

Media Liaison Plan

Organizations depending on the news media to communicate information to the public often have misunderstandings about the needs of journalists, their roles and the most efficient ways to interact with news organizations. One of these misconceptions is that media people don't show enough initiative. Organizations which depend upon wide and general support need the reporters to transmit information through the media to various stakeholders.

It is the newsmaker's responsibility to be understood, not the news writer's responsibility to understand.

Newspeople work with the distractions of talking, keyboarding, wire services, radio, television and police scanners going most of the time. They are often besieged by hundreds of phone calls and news releases each week. If an organization's message is not clear and newsworthy, it will not become news. If it does not communicate with all significant media people in its market, reporters will not generally seek out the organization to see if there is something newsworthy that a spokesperson might have to say. It is not sufficient simply to be available should a media person call, since there are hundreds of other legitimate news sources that a reporter might contact on any given day.

This communication posture is in keeping with strategy of being "message driven" rather than "question driven" or active versus merely re-active.

It is not sufficient to send one press release to every newsroom in the community and assume that every reporter is aware of it. It is a mistake to assume that a press release sent to a wire service will be passed on to newspapers and electronic members of the network. If the editor does not think the press release is newsworthy, it is not put on the wire. However, if a member media outlet also receives that press release it could well be considered newsworthy by another editor. The paid wires may not be accessed by all columnists, editorial writers and others.

Similarly, if a press release is sent to "The Editor" at a newspaper or a radio station, it is a mistake to assume that the press release is passed on to program hosts, interviewers, columnists, talk show hosts, morning show producers and others.

While this may sound inefficient, it is the reality of the media. Thus, the most effective thing for the organization to do is to take responsibility for communicating with a much wider range of journalists in the community. The Media Liaison Plan is one method of doing this (See Appendix 3, Figure 3.2).

This draft offers some examples of how to systematically communicate with a variety of people in the print and electronic media. One event or interaction per month with reporters can be planned this way.

There are commercial lists of media outlets that can be purchased and kept up to date semi-annually, as should a list of other media people with whom the organization comes into contact.

Most television markets have morning interview shows. Note the time in the lower right hand corner. For me to be on-air at 6:57, I had to get up at 5:30. Here I am shoulder to shoulder and knee to knee with someone I've just met. This can make for a challenging morning for anyone.

Chapter 4   Get Set

Now you know what you want to say, who should say it and which news organizations you'd like to approach to deliver your fascinating story to an eager public. Far too many would-be media players think this is all they need to make a splash that will be noticed far and wide.

But there's more to be done before you take the plunge. Lot's more.

It's time for you to draw on the lessons learned and used by all great communicators. You can never know enough about the other side.

Understanding the Media

It is remarkable given the prevalence of the news media in today's society that so many people remain so ignorant of journalist's work methods, motivations and requirements.

Simply put, the news media are in the business of selling advertising by attracting the attention of as many people as possible. Different outlets go about doing this in different ways, but apart from public or semi-public media (i.e. the Canadian Broadcasting Corporation, the British Broadcasting Corporation or the Public Broadcasting System in the US) they are all concerned with making a profit.

News outlets collect and disseminate news at a phenomenal rate. Reporter's are expected to produce numerous stories quickly, accurately and interestingly. The difficulty or ease with which the reporter gathers information to produce the story can and does have an enormous bearing on the final product.

We all like to cheer heroes and curse villains, and the news media try to satisfy our appetites. In their zeal to do so they sometimes get it wrong. It may be that the reporter misunderstood, spoke to the wrong person or just didn't have the right information available.

Most people take the view that it's the reporter's responsibility to "get it right" and that's all there is to it. But that doesn't do much good if, for whatever reason, the reporter gets it wrong and your image, reputation or business is affected. You can complain, and even seek redress through the courts if you feel the damage is serious enough. But that takes time. Meanwhile your image remains tarnished in the minds of your customers, stakeholders and the public at large.

This is why organizations should take an active part in the process when they find themselves in the spotlight and reporters are interested in their activities. Think of yourself as a participant rather than a victim. Find out more about the other team and learn the rules of the game.

You may like the media. You may detest it. It really doesn't matter. The only thing that counts is how well you are prepared to deal with the media and its representatives if and when you come into contact with them.

The first thing to remember is that reporters, editors, photographers, producers etc. are just like the rest of us. With few exceptions they need a regular paycheque to feed, clothe and house themselves and their dependents. And apart from those who work at senior levels in the big national broadcast organizations, national magazines or big city newspapers, they are not very well paid.

To climb the ladder and reach those better paid positions they have to stand out and be noticed. This explains — in part — the determination (and sometimes aggression) that media folk display when chasing a story. It's an expensive business to dispatch reporters and camera crews to check up on story tips and no editor likes to see a reporter come back empty-handed. Reporters quickly learn to find something interesting to say about an event — no matter how mundane or insignificant that event may be to everyone else.

With that in mind, let's take a brief look at some of the elements that go into the making of a typical story.

A television news story (and TV is where most of us get our news from) may appear to be short and simple, but it is not simple. The diagram of "A Reporter's Building Blocks" (Page 50) gives you an idea of how a fairly common TV story is constructed.

The newscaster introduces the item. The scene is set with voice-over narration of visuals (b-roll or cover footage) leading to public reaction. This could be protesters, neighbours, or people passing by. The third party expert could be a professor, lawyer or other authority figure. The folk hero is someone who has become involved either through personal experience or by witnessing the actual event. Sound clips, archival visuals and the reporter appearing on camera to make her summation fill out the rest of the item.

If you are the newsmaker you can be squeezed between any two of these building blocks. And you won't have much time to make your point. It is a statistical fact that the average length of time devoted to your remarks in a television news item, when there's controversy, is just 8 seconds. With feature items, you might get up to 20 seconds and in a relaxed interview format you might get 45 seconds. That isn't long, so you have to be good. However, if you are good you can have a huge influence on how the item finally emerges from the editing suite.

Reporters and editors are more likely to use clips of people who know what they're talking about and can explain issues briefly than those who don't and can't. They make choices and you can affect their choice.

A print news story is constructed like an inverted pyramid. Instead of building from a broad base to a pointed conclusion, its starts with the end result and moves on to specific details.

"Hundreds of people are homeless today on the Yucatan Peninsula" is a typical opening statement, or lead, for a newspaper story. Later, you get the causes and additional details. There was a storm, boats were capsized and homes destroyed. It may have been the worst storm in history. Eyewitnesses said they were "shocked" at the devastation and emergency workers are on the scene.

Now if you were an emergency worker who just happened to be on the scene you may not figure very prominently in the story at this early stage. The inverted pyramid approach assumes that all the important components are close to the top and less important aspects are lower down. Editors working under deadline pressures can cut from the bottom of the story to fit a certain length without distorting the sense of the story.

However, your message and demeanour can influence whether you are depicted as peripheral or central to the story. The reporter could just as easily start this way: "Fast action by emergency crews is the best hope for hundreds of homeless people on the Yucatan Peninsula." The rest of the story is the same but the focus is now on a remedy not the problem.

A REPORTER'S BUILDING BLOCKS

Here are two versions of the same news story. The first is an example of a straight, matter-of-fact report reflecting the situation as the reporter sees it with very little input from emergency workers on the scene:

Hundreds of people are homeless today on the Yucatan peninsula. A major tropical storm destroyed about 100 homes and capsized dozens of fishing and pleasure boats overnight. One local tourist operator is Frank Smith, originally from London, Ontario, now managing the Beachfront Yacht Club. Mr. Smith says it's the worst storm anyone remembers in the area. Local aid workers are marshalling volunteers and trying to erect temporary housing. So far, there are no reports of any deaths.

If this were a radio story, the reporter might include background sound of wind, workers yelling or bulldozers clearing roads, as well as an audio clip of Frank Smith. For TV there would be appropriate visuals. The second version contains the same facts but shifts the emphasis because the reporter had the time and inclination to talk to you — a knowledgeable and articulate emergency worker armed with the appropriate SOCKOs:

Luckily some of the first people on the scene after a destructive storm hit the Yucatan Peninsula last night were a dozen aid workers from several different humanitarian organizations. Many were on their first assignment and had only been away from home a few weeks. But all moved swiftly into high gear to try to find hundreds of homeless after the tropical storm destroyed about 100 houses and capsized dozens of fishing and pleasure boats. The aid workers were on the scene before dawn and used bull horns and lanterns to try to round up the missing. Ironically, one from Canada, Sue Jones of Halifax, found fellow Canadian Frank Smith from London, who now manages the Beachfront Yacht Club. He was fine and quickly joined the search for some of his guests. So far there are no reports of any deaths.

Imagine the impact on the boards of the aid organizations involved, those who fund them and recruiters after story number two appears versus story number one. Both are legitimate coverage, but from different angles.

You may think the above turn-around is wishful thinking. However, I developed this strategy and the above example after extensive work with international diplomats and aid workers. They have achieved, in real situations around the world, exactly the kind of shift of focus I advocate. Some of the situations involved serious injury and death, not just homeless visitors and tourist operators.

Newspeople

There are so many references to "the media" today that it's easy to think of it as some sort of powerful, inanimate object rather than individuals doing different jobs for different organizations, some small, some large, some good and some bad. Even the term "journalist" can be misleading because it can refer to almost anyone in the news business. So it might be helpful for us to take a look at some of the different job categories to be found in the news media.

Reporters are at the sharp end of the business. They're the people who go out and collect the information, either in person, over the phone or via the Internet, and write the original stories. As a newsmaker, it is reporters with whom you are most likely to have contact. Correspondent is just a fancy name for reporter.

Some reporters have specialized areas of responsibility i.e. politics, crime, education, health, science, environment, sports, business, technology, entertainment etc. The bigger the news organization the more specialists it will have. These specialized areas are sometimes called "beats." If you are being interviewed by a beat reporter, you can expect a more knowledgeable line of questioning because that person is focused on fewer topics than a general reporter.

News organizations have been affected by the same economic and technological changes that have buffeted the business world in general over the past two decades. They too are struggling to cope with downsizing, multi-tasking, convergence and cross-ownership. A company that owns radio and television outlets as well as a major newspaper in one area will often seek to "maximize efficiencies" by getting double duty out of its reporters — meaning there are fewer reporters and they have less time to research and prepare their stories.

Print reporters are often accompanied by photographers and television reporters can be accompanied by "crews" of different sizes, depending on the complexity of the "shoot" and the size and professionalism of the station or network involved.

Don't forget these people are also part of the news business and should be treated as such. They may want to give the impression they are not in the same business as the reporter digging for facts, but don't be fooled! Any careless or unscripted comments you make to them will quickly be passed on.

Be as professional and polite to the photographers and technicians as you are to the reporters, hosts and interviewers. It may not be obvious to you, but they all have a role to play in the way you and your story, or message, will be seen and heard by an audience.

Columnists, unlike reporters, are expected to express their opinions. Sometimes reporters also write columns. In fact anyone can be a columnist. They may be syndicated, meaning their work is made widely available through an agency, or strictly local. Some will write only on topics about which they are expert, others will ramble on about anything they want.

Columnists are free to "dip" in and out of stories whenever they wish. They're under no obligation to tell a story from beginning to end. They can take one aspect or a story, or a single quote from you or anyone else, and use it in a completely different context. So if you happen to be talking to one, try to find out just what kind of columnist you're dealing with.

Dealing with a well-known, opinionated person who happens to write a column can be more of a challenge than dealing with a general reporter. Columnists may also make speeches, write books, lecture or engage in any number of other activities to round out their income. But the same basic rules apply. Do your homework. Have SOCKOs ready and practise them. Be respectful of the columnist's time, make your case and ask for support. Above all, remember that everything you do and say is "on the record."

Outside the mainstream news media there are trade journals. Many industrial sectors and business areas have publications catering specifically to their interests. As you'd expect, the reporters who work on these journals are usually more knowledgeable about your business or industry than reporters in the general news media. However, that doesn't automatically mean tougher interviews.

Trade journals have more limited sources of revenue than the mainstream media. They depend on subscriptions and advertising from the very people they are writing about so they tend to accentuate the positive. Nonetheless, prepare as you would for any other specialty reporter. Articles about you and your business in a trade journal may be good to reproduce and send to employees, customers, suppliers, neighbours and even the mainstream media. Trade journals may be a first step in enhancing your reputation.

Editor is another generalized term, like journalist. It requires a modifier before it makes any sense — although you can be reasonably sure these people work "inside" and rarely go to the scene of the action and therefore have less direct contact with the public.

In newspapers you'll find:

> copy editors, who may check and rewrite reporters' stories or the material from news agencies
> city editors and their assistants who decide which local stories will be covered and how they will be presented, or "played"
> picture or photo editors
> foreign editors, editorial page editors, features editors, sports editors etc., all working under the direction of the managing editors

In radio and television newsrooms you could find:

> assignment editors, who assign the stories to be covered
> researchers, who really are reporters in everything but name
> copy and story editors who polish the raw material
> line-up editors or program producers who pick the items that go in the newscast or program
> producers of various sorts who all have some influence on editorial content.

Many news organizations will list their key editorial people and specialist reporters and columnists on their web sites. You may find some interested in you and your activities. However, it's always advisable to have some idea of the role of the person you are talking to. If the job title doesn't help, ask for an explanation!

The Changing Media

I began writing news on a typewriter. In our small and cheap broadcasting station we cut audio tape with a razor blade and even edited silent, negative film by ripping out black spots with our fingers and splicing the two pieces back together with ordinary, clear, sticky tape! You don't have to be an expert to appreciate the problems this could cause as the film ran over the sprockets in the projector.

Technology affected how we covered the news in those days.

It still does.

Computers let us be writers as well as editors. We can block and move, search and replace, spell check and grammar check after we write instead of having to think about the story before we begin writing. Laptops allow us to do all this in the field and transmit the story back to the newsroom almost instantaneously.

Editing digital audio on a computer is quicker and more accurate than working with tape. Radio reporters and producers can include quotes and clips from five different time zones with a click of the mouse. In the past the raw tape would be shipped in by bus or plane or "fed" in by telephone or broadcast quality audio line (the Cadillac option).

Videotape replaced film in newscasts years ago and digital editing is now so smooth that it has raised concerns that perhaps you should not always believe what you see! Faxes, modems and wireless handheld communicators allow newspaper reporters to check wire stories and the competition before filing stories.

When I was Executive Assistant to a big city Mayor in the 1980s, I'd regularly mail news releases to the media with great effect. Paid wire services didn't have the reach and faxes weren't yet in widespread use. Today, if you ask a panel of reporters at a conference how they want you to reach them, you'll get many different answers: through my producer, my cell phone, the newsroom phone, fax, email, wireless handheld communicators and so on.

The first course I taught was called "Mass Media Studies." Soon afterwards, I regularly gave a speech to The Canadian Police College called "the Death of the Mass Media." I was making a point about the fragmentation of the market, proliferation of stations and the multiple choices that consumers had.

Today, the market is more fragmented and diverse — and tomorrow it will be even more so. New digital technology allows broadcasters to use the frequencies assigned to them to carry several television or radio channels, plus a variety of other data services.

When you consider that each television station will be able to transmit as many as five different signals and add that to the choices already available via cable and satellite, you have some idea how much the broadcast scene is changing. And we haven't included "streaming" on the Internet. However, more choice of news outlets to watch, listen to or read may not automatically mean more reporters or more varied sources of information.

Through convergence and cross-ownership the same media companies today often own newspapers, radio stations, TV stations, magazines as well as Internet providers. That means fewer sources of news, even if there are more news outlets and appliances on which to access it.

Owners of news outlets are looking to maintain their earnings by collecting smaller amounts, but from many more outlets. They can't afford to let each small outlet run its own news operation. That may well lead to shared newsrooms and fewer reporters and staff trying to cover the same geographic area.

If you are a public affairs professional, you need to keep up with these changes and trends. What worked well in the first part of your career just might be obsolete in the second half.

The other major change involves the "face" of the media. When I began reporting, the business was dominated by white males. Women were just being hired in greater numbers and people of colour were not yet well-represented. All that is changing.

Medium and large-sized cities throughout North America are attracting immigrants and refugees at an incredible rate. The Greater Toronto Area (the largest urban area in Canada) is absorbing 70,000 immigrants and refugees every year, of whom 40% speak neither English nor French. Projections based on census data show that almost one half of the area's population of five million people now consists of ethnic minorities and the figure is growing at an annual rate of 1.5%.

All sorts of new publications and broadcasting stations are being established to cater to a growing appetite for news and entertainment in languages other than English, French or Spanish. Some operate in one language and culture, others may be shared by several ethnic minorities. However they all have viewers and listeners who are consumers and who, eventually, will take their place in the social and political life of their communities.

Advertisers are already aware of these new opportunities. People interested in good media relations should also be aware of the additional opportunities provided by these outlets to tell their stories. Making an effort now may pay off later.

Chapter 5   Go!

Working with the Media

There's no guarantee that being knowledgeable about and cooperative with the media will bring you favourable coverage. But, there's no doubt that using professional techniques will give you more opportunities to influence that coverage.

A Communications Matrix and Media Liaison Plan will help you identify useful media contacts and keep in touch with them. You need to develop their confidence so they feel comfortable in turning to you as an information resource.

Having a clearly defined point of view or an area of particular expertise is invaluable. So is an ability to deliver quotable statements in a timely fashion. Just remember that reporters won't give you an opportunity to strut your stuff without a good reason. The reason may not always be clear to you but if you are properly prepared and rehearsed your involvement should enhance your reputation.

Even if you've had a bad experience dealing with the media in the past, don't give up. Keep searching for areas of common interest with news outlets and their reporters. You never know where it could lead.

What follows is detailed and practical advice on the various forms of contact you may have with the news media.

Media Kit

A good media kit helps provide a solid foundation for relations with the media. This is where you get to set out your story, the background, salient points and supporting facts without being interrupted — and in the way you want it to be seen.

While it is unlikely this material will ever be used in its entirety by reporters it can be a useful resource for them when they are battling deadlines, or when they are looking for interesting snippets of information to flesh-out their story.

A basic kit should contain:

> A brief history of the organization, company or enterprise, a chronology of significant dates and photographs of significant features (i.e. head office, main plant, main product or activity)
> Biographies and photographs of the principals
> Fact sheet(s) listing the organization's statistics – employees, number and weight of widgets produced annually, number of countries importing widgets etc.

This basic kit can then be augmented with more information and background to meet more specific needs. It can even be augmented with appropriate sound and video material to meet the needs of broadcast journalists.

However, resist the temptation to stuff the kit full of any and all publicity material generated by the company or institution in the previous years. Reporters trying to meet a deadline don't have time to read the speech given by the CEO to the Board of Trade last fall. If time is an important factor for reporters receiving the kit, make sure the material it contains is relevant.

These kits can be handed out at news conferences, briefings and one-on-one interviews — or sent directly to news organization and their reporters who are unable to be present at your media event. You'll find many uses for a professional media kit. You may use some of the material in investor relations, with neighbours, customers or new employees. If you have a good web site, you may not need many hard copies of the kit. Simply direct interested parties to your organization's web address.

Following is an example of a media kit as it might apply to my own company:

ALLAN BONNER COMMUNICATIONS MANAGEMENT INC.
Phone 1-877-484-1667
e-mail allan@allanbonner.com
www.allanbonner.com

We Prepare You For The Unthinkable!

We develop and deliver customized training in risk, crisis and disaster management for corporate executives, public sector officials and spokespeople for vital institutions and organizations.

Allan, his trainers and consultants, have all been working journalists in some of the top news rooms of the world. They know the news business from the inside. You may remember some of them from The National News, Morningside, the major daily newspapers, the RKO radio networks and reports from 70 countries and hot spots around the world. Several are fluent in French. They are the reporters you'd be trying to reach if they'd stayed in the business. But now they work for you.

Company History

Allan Bonner Communications Management Incorporated started in the mid-1980s as Allan Bonner and Associates, which provided media training to corporate executives at Seneca College's Conference Centre in Toronto.

In 1987 the Department of National Defence retained the company to help senior officers at DND Headquarters in Ottawa and military bases across the country to deal with the contentious issues of cruise missile testing and the potential purchase of nuclear submarines. Other early clients included major oil and gas companies, a national lobby group, one of the country's largest law firms and a leading polling company.

Since that time the company has added trainers and additional services to help clients better. In 2000 the company established The Centre for Training in Risk and Crisis Management in down-town Toronto. The Centre features a large training room, break-out rooms, four radio and TV studios, an extensive library and is fully wired with coaxial cable for video training.

Courses offered by Allan Bonner Communications Management Inc. include:

[LIST RELEVANT INFORMATION]

Clients

Our work frequently exposes us to highly sensitive and confidential information and where necessary, client confidentiality is assured.

In the past, however, our clients have included governments in North America, Europe, Asia and the Caribbean as well as the United Nations, NATO, major international banks and companies in the energy, aerospace and pharmaceutical sectors.

[LIST RELEVANT INFORMATION]

Facts and Figures

In the past 20 years, Allan Bonner Communications Management Inc. has trained more than 15,000 people, including six heads of government, eight party leaders, thirty cabinet ministers, dozens of ambassadors and hundreds of other diplomats.

Training seminars have been conducted in thirteen countries on five continents. Sites include: Hong Kong, Seoul, Tokyo, Bangkok, Beijing, Singapore, Canberra, Budapest, Geneva, Bled, Dubai, Bermuda, Brussels and major cities across North America.

Allan Bonner is often interviewed by television and radio programs and is frequently invited to address professional and public events. Recent media appearances include:

[LIST RELEVANT INFORMATION]

Biographies

[LIST KEY ORGANIZATION'S MEMBERS INFORMATION]

Writing News Releases

A news release ("press release" pre-dates broadcast journalism) can be an effective way of reaching a large number of reporters quickly. Reporters prefer one-on-one interviews and other direct means of collecting their own information but they will refer to news releases for basic facts, background information and to find out the individual's or organization's point of view.

Some small, community-based news organizations will run news releases just as they receive them (and sometimes even as their own story!). Most news outlets do not. They are inundated with news releases every day, most of which get short shrift from journalists looking for something that will impress their editors and, eventually, the public.

The biggest single reason for news releases being ignored is that they miss their targets. They're sifted by the wrong people. A release announcing a new production technique for widgets is unlikely to elicit much excitement on the news desk of a major metropolitan news outlet.

However it may be of interest to the technology reporter. So try to direct your release to the right audience and then follow up with a phone call to see if that person or department has seen it.

If you are unsure where to send your releases check your local or national media directories. These are usually published annually and are available electronically as well as in public libraries. To reach a large number of news outlets quickly you can use the services of an electronic distribution service.

If you want your news release to be worth a second look, you have to frame it in such a way that it will attract a journalist's attention. Collect the facts by asking the traditional journalistic questions WHO, WHEN, WHAT, WHERE, WHY and HOW (See Appendix 3, Figure 3.5).

The next step is to ask yourself:
> Who will benefit?
> What is being done?
> What is new?
> When will results show?
> Where will the greatest impact be?
> Why is this being done?

There's bad news, good news and bad news again in the use of news releases.

The bad news is that most public affairs practitioners report how tough it is to get their story placed in the media. The other side of that coin, though, is that media people are often scrambling for something to use each day. That's the good news. In addition, the number of media outlets at which you can pitch your releases is growing.

In Canada alone, there are over 100 TV stations, about 1700 conventional AM and FM radio stations, almost 1000 daily and weekly newspapers and about the same number of business magazines and other publications. If you throw in cable television (Canada is about the most cabled country in the world), free newspapers and community flyers- then add the proximity of US media across the border — you will see there is no end to opportunity. Although there is a lot of competition for news space, if your approach is professional, you have a great chance of success.

Let me explain. At one point in my career, I hosted an afternoon talk and interview show and was always looking for something to put on the air. I'd interview a couple of authors a week, follow a few news stories and expand them into interviews and then the fear would set in. What if I didn't have enough items for the day's show?

I'd often turn to a file folder of news releases I kept. These hadn't been judged worthy of a news story in their own right but I kept them handy just in case I ran short of material in the studio. Many of these releases consisted of solid blocks of words — margin to margin prose and single spaced. I'd throw them away because I didn't have the time to delve into the mysteries they concealed.

Some were unusable because they didn't carry dates so I had no idea of their "shelf life." Others were interesting, but either failed to list a contact person or the contact person didn't return my calls.

Sometimes I'd talk to three or four people in a company who had no idea of what their own release was all about! Then there was one telling me how proud John Smith was to receive this year's Minipie Award — but no indication what the award was for. More garbage. It was a real struggle to find a usable news release in the pile.

So, the really good news is that if you use the standard format I advocate in this book, call ahead to alert the producer — and call to follow up. You have a good chance of getting on air or in the newspaper.

However, if you are going to send out a news release announcing an event, or if you are trying to get publicity for your cause by making yourself or a spokesperson available for an interview, make sure you have done your homework so that both you and the news outlet know what to expect.

Most journalists have horror stories to tell about inept or incorrect communications that can cause red faces all round. Michael Enright of CBC Radio's "Sunday Morning" once launched into a live interview with the leader of a group of Buddhist Monks, only to discover the man did not speak a word of English! He smiled a lot, but this was of little benefit to the radio audience who were left wondering why this interview consisted only of questions! Eventually a junior member of the group indicated that he could act as interpreter.

My favourite story on this topic comes from my wife, Lorna Jackson, a CBC interviewer and program host, whose work has also been on NPR in the US. She was host of a program called "The Food Show" on the CBC network and would often get media releases and announcements from some of the largest public relations agencies in the world. They'd send her glossy pictures of butter or some other product, and pages of background material. Just what she was supposed to do with pictures on a radio show remains a mystery.

Publicists would also send her cookbooks, then phone her and ask if she intended to interview the authors. When she declined they'd ask,

"Why not?" stressing the virtues of the recipes, the charm of the author or health virtues of the diet. Lorna would reply the book did not really fall into the mandate of the show. Had the publicists bothered to listen to the program they would have known that it dealt with international food aid, the political economy of food and food public policy. A recipe book had no business on this show!

I also failed the homework test with one of my first news releases. I thought I had it made when I prepared a release for a charitable organization that was opening a building to house needy and disabled people. I was sure it would make the newscasts as a feel-good "kicker," or last item on one of the local newscasts.

However, on that very same day:

Mila Mulroney, wife of Canada's Prime Minister had a baby, while her husband was celebrating the first anniversary of his government taking office.

Lincoln Alexander became the first black man to be appointed Lieutenant-Governor of Ontario.

There were major developments in municipal politics.

A popular theatrical troupe that includes the mentally handicapped in its productions opened an engagement at a local theatre.

My story didn't make the news that night. I should have found out more about the news competition my client was facing that day.

An Analysis of Newsworthiness

Reporters are in constantly evaluating the newsworthiness of information that surrounds them. They hear gossip and stories. They read newspapers and magazines. They often have a radio or TV on in the newsroom while they are working. They constantly check wire services and the web. All the while there's a mental weigh scale operating in their minds. If this scale tips to one side, then the information is probably interesting, useful and important enough to make it in the news. If not, it's in the garbage. But how is this decision made? A lot of it is instinct, but I've tried to make the decision as scientific as possible (See Appendix 3, Figure 3.3).

Across the top of the chart are just a few of the considerations a journalist will use in judging whether your story gets in the news. Generally, a story is more newsworthy the newer it is. Stories from close to home are more important than ones from far away. If your item affects a lot of people and is of lasting importance, that could be news. If this big change is widespread, then that's even more newsworthy. There exceptions, and more categories, but this should get you thinking along the right lines.

Then all this data is filtered through the traditional journalistic questions — Who, What, When, Where, Why and How — the 5Ws and the "H" as they're sometimes called. You can use these too. If you ask yourself or your spokesperson these questions, the exercise will help you gather all the relevant information about the story. You might ask ten "who" questions, five "what" questions and so on down the list. You may not have the journalistic instinct developed after writing thousands of stories, but you have an inquiring mind and more technical information than the journalist.

By using this grid it is clear that stories are much more newsworthy when they are brand new, nearby, affect many people, have lasting historical importance or are a pivotal point in the history of an event, organization or movement.

Leads

News stories flow in a certain way. In journalistic jargon, there's a focus. A focus might be "the new workfare program doesn't work," or "the police budget is out of control." That focus sets a tone and helps the journalist decide what information to include in the story, and what to throw out. In the police budget story, you probably wouldn't include information on how dangerous police work is, unless the budget involves buying bullet-proof vests.

A hook is a reason for doing a particular story in this newscast. A hook really requires that a story be used today, because tomorrow it will be out of date. The police news hook might be the start of a new fiscal year. It might also be that the matter came up at City Council. After you've decided you have a hook, you need a lead, or first sentence that gets you going. After than you tell the story. Your story involves details and reactions from people, as any good story does.

The lead is probably the most important part of the process. The major rule is to make it interesting.

The first decision in writing a news release involves the first sentence or "lead." The only absolute rule is that you should try to make it interesting. After that you can take any number of approaches, providing the tone and content are appropriate to the situation. Here are some suggestions:

An "umbrella" lead is an all encompassing overview of a situation — the big picture.
> EXAMPLE: Consumers in thirteen states are worried about potato prices.

A "rifle" lead focuses on one small emblematic aspect of a situation.
> EXAMPLE: Nobody likes french fries more than 12-year-old Amy Bloggins.

A "historical" lead would begin with events past and lead up to the present.
> EXAMPLE: Ever since scientists developed a hearty strain of potatoes, french fries have been popular here.

A "geographic" lead would indicate the effect over a wide area.
> EXAMPLE: The whole eastern seaboard is concerned about potato blight.

The type of lead chosen will dictate the tone and methodology for the rest of the release. For example, when you use a historical lead, the rest of the news release will likely contain a chronology of events and data leading to the current situation.

Whichever method is used, some general rules always apply:
> Communicate one thought per sentence
> Write in the present tense
> Use the active voice ("I hit the ball." Not, "The ball was hit by me.")

Transmit simple word pictures in short sentences (no longer than 18 words). Tell a story simply and clearly.

You should continually ask yourself "who cares?" If you cannot picture a nurse, police officer, taxi driver, labourer, professor, or neighbour being interested, then it is unlikely to be considered news by an editor.

Hooks

News hooks are a journalist's reasons for doing a story. Unusual things, human interest and striking photographs are special cases where the hook may be the story itself. Generally though, a news release must have an implied reason for use by the news outlet.

Other obvious hooks include the national implications of local stories, local angles to international stories, notable developments in continuing stories and the organization's reaction to stories. The news release should be written so that an editor cannot put it away for review or possible use another day or another week. It should have compelling reasons for immediate use.

Press Release Format

> Leave generous margins all around
> Use your organization's stationery
> Remove mundane, procedural data and get quickly into the head line and body
> Type "For Immediate Release" or "Not for release before 2 p.m." and the date in the upper right hand corner or in the dateline
> Use a short, grabby headline typed in capitals
> Write in a conversational, journalistic style (use a style book)
> Avoid boring details-start with a quote, list dates, places and other details further down
> Double or triple space
> End with the traditional marks, -30- , which signify the end of a story
> Name a contact person and provide a phone number at the end
> Attach something, prepare a kit with biographies of key people, chronologies, background, pictures

Following is a sample media release:

[INSERT LETTERHEAD HEADERS HERE]

ATTENTION NEWS EDITORS   *FOR IMMEDIATE RELEASE*

CAN YOU SURVIVE A MEDIA MARATHON?

March 15, 2003 — TORONTO, ONTARIO — Communications professionals can learn how to get their message across in a 12-hour, intensive, Media Marathon conducted by Allan Bonner Communications. The marathon starts on March 21 at 6 a.m. Your communications skills will be tested in a variety of situations, from radio and television interviews, to scrums and press conferences.

The event will be led by experienced trainers and former journalists Allan Bonner, Hal Jones, Joe Coté and Larry Solway. They will simulate shows they actually hosted, produced and lined-up such as: Metro Morning, Ontario Morning, Morningside, Radio Noon, Open Line, Talk Radio, the 6:00 Evening News and As It Happens. In addition, participants can see their interviews written up in print and critiqued by an editorial team.

Based on Allan Bonner's critically acclaimed book, as well as the SOCKO Training System, the session will help you learn what to say, how you say it and how journalists will react.

Bonner has over 15 years of experience in media training and crisis management, with over 15,000 senior executives, Fortune 500 CEOs and their staffs, government officials and diplomats around the world. He has worked with such organizations as the WTO, NATO the UN and G7 Summits.

The March 21 training session will be held at the Centre for Training in Risk and Crisis Management. The fee is $1,200.00 per participant and bookings can be made by calling 1-877-484-1667.

- 30 -

For more information, call toll free 1-877-484-1667.
E-mail: allan@allanbonner.com

Chapter 6   Face-to-Face

Sending out media releases, fact sheets and other prepared materials is a good way to start. However, apart from paid advertisements, trade or community-based publications, you will find very few people in the news business who will just take your words and use them the way you intended.

Reporters like to report and editors like to edit. So if your release generates some interest with the media, you can expect phone calls from news people asking all sorts of questions. The questions may be factual, suggestive, off-base, pointed or argumentative. How you respond will have a direct bearing on whether your media release gets tossed in the waste basket, is filed for future reference or used as the basis for a feature article on you.

What follows is a detailed guide to help you deal with news people when you meet them face-to-face, over the phone — or even "live" on air. Remember, too, that you don't have to send out a media release to attract media attention. Depending on your interests, your business or your proximity to a big news story, you could get a phone call at any time.

When a Reporter Calls:
> Ask for some "think" time
> Take notes
> Ask "what is your deadline?"
> Find out who they represent
> Find out if they are the journalist, researcher or producer
> Ask what the segment or article will be about
> Discover what approach they are taking
> Ask what research, reports and documents have been seen? Offer your own
> Ask what areas of discussion they would like to cover?
> Find out where the interview will take place
> Ask who else will be interviewed?

> Discover date of airing or publication
> Ask how long the interview will last?
> Ask yourself the outcome if you do not cooperate
> Be prepared to tape the conversation

Always call the reporter back. If you decide you are not the best person to deal with the issue, call the reporter and say so. If you can suggest an alternative, so much the better.

How to Be a Good News Source:
> Help build the story
> Prepare, rehearse out loud
> Be convincing, not combative
> Have the audience think well of you
> Grab the good words, good concepts and moral high ground for yourself
> Never forget you're talking to a journalist – it's not a conversation
> Stay cool and firm
> Show caring, knowledge and action

Interviews

By and large this is the preferred method for reporters to collect their information about people and events.

Apart from the "I-was-there" type of story, most journalism involves reporting on events from the perspective of a third party. Interviews with people central to the story allow the reporter to get the information first-hand. They can then use the words of eye witnesses to help make the rest of us understand what it was like to be at the scene, or to understand what happened or how others reacted.

Be careful not to get carried away with hyperbole or sentiment. You may want to emulate the "hype" used by tabloid journalism, but even that material is carefully vetted. One cautionary tale told in newsrooms years ago concerned a keen young reporter sent to cover a train crash who phoned in a story beginning: "God sat on a hilltop today and wept as two, crowded passenger trains collided head-on in the valley below."

Within a few minutes his editor came on the line and barked: "Forget the train crash — interview God!"

When a reporter calls, let him or her know you are willing to provide them with information (so long as you are the right person!). Then try to determine what information they require. They won't give you their questions in advance but they will tell you the general area of interest. Find out what kind of deadline pressure the reporter is facing and then assure him you will call back as soon as you can. This will provide you with some "think time" on how best to respond to the reporter's questions.

When you do call the reporter back, you can establish some control over the proceedings by setting a time limit for the interview.

Always assume your conversations with reporters are on the record, both figuratively and literally. Some news organization have strict rules that reporters must tell the other person if the conversation is being recorded — others do not. Legal requirements also vary among jurisdictions. Find out what applies to you.

In Canada, anyone can record his own conversations with others, face-to-face or on the phone, without having to tell the other person. However, if reporters intend to broadcast any part of that conversation on the radio, they have to get the other party's permission. Strangely, this prohibition does not extend to broadcasting the recorded conversation on television!

In practice, this means that reporters don't have to tell you they are recording your words unless they intend to broadcast it on the radio.

You can also take advantage of this law. Politicians usually make sure they have their own copy of an interview or other contact with the media and public and so should you.

I'm always surprised when clients ask: "But won't reporters object?" There's nothing to object to! And it serves notice to reporters that you are approaching the interview in a professional manner. Should a dispute arise later about what exactly was said, the reporter won't have the only version of the recorded interview.

Case Study

A few years ago I received a phone call in my office from a well known reporter with a big city Canadian daily newspaper who asked if I was Allan Bonner, the media trainer.

I told him my media training was only one of several different courses and services offered by my company.

What came out of the phone next was not a question, but a dollar figure (a big one) and the name of a Federal Government Department, which happens to be a long-standing client of mine: "X thousand dollars . . . Z ministry . . ." his voice trailed off to nothing.

Yikes! My heart rate increased and a number of thoughts flashed through my mind. I couldn't talk about my client. The dollar figure wasn't exactly right but may have been for a different year.

I asked a series of questions to try to find out why the journalist was so interested in me. He was under no obligation to tell me, of course, but the more I could find out, the safer I'd be. He may have just gotten up on the wrong side of the bed, or he may have just had the normal journalist's skepticism about anyone who helps people deal with reporters. All he'd tell me was that he had made "freedom of information" requests of the government to find out how much work I'd done and how much I had been paid. I asked what year he was talking about. It was three years prior.

I said: "Even a small company like mine uses an accountant to prepare and submit billings so I'll have to check . . . ."

"But you'd have a rough idea, wouldn't you?" the reporter interrupted.

"I might," I responded, "But I also have confidentiality agreements with clients, so I can't confirm or discuss who is or who isn't a client, let alone what I billed them."

My predicament was that while I was constrained from talking about my clients, experience told me it is dangerous not to be able to tell journalists something when they have you in their sights. I had to get a little more control and be less intransigent. So I tried offering some information and shifted gears to asking questions.

I said: "If I get written permission from my client to discuss this with you I will. Otherwise all I can do is confirm that I do a lot of work in Ottawa and have worked for most government departments and many public agencies."

I then began asking questions:

"What do you know about my business?"

"Have you seen any of our materials?"

"What kinds of information can I provide you."

"When is your deadline?"

I found out that the reporter was doing the story for the weekend, so I had a little time. I offered to fax him some information about the company and agreed to an interview based on that information later in the day. During our exchange I learned some of the areas of my business that interested him so as soon as we'd hung up I prepared some general information on those areas. I included that in the package of faxed information along with my bio, some news clippings and some articles I'd written.

I called my friend David Potts, a libel lawyer and media specialist, to get his opinion on what the reporter might be after. He confirmed what I'd suspected: that reporters are suspicious of anything that smacks of media spin or manipulation — and media training for government officials raises that possibility. His view is that journalists see media training as an unwelcome filter between them and their sources of information.

But then I had another idea. If this reporter wanted to investigate my business, he might just be interested in talking to my competitors. There's only one in Ottawa, and as I'd met him before I felt quite comfortable phoning him to tell him he could be hearing from this reporter. I was too late. He'd already been interviewed!

However, I learned that a major thrust of the reporter's questioning was whether the government had sent either of us abroad to conduct training sessions. The reporter had it in his mind that while the government paid for the overseas trip, the trainer would be able to piggyback sessions for private sector clients. In other words, taxpayers were subsidizing the private sector.

I was more exposed on this issue because it was I, not my competitor, who had conducted training sessions in Asia, the US and Europe for two different government departments. But the reporter had the story backwards. It was my overseas clients who mainly paid my travel costs, allowing me also to train Canadian government officials in Hong Kong, Beijing, Seoul, Tokyo and Canberra for about the same cost as if the sessions had been conducted in Ottawa.

I now had more information about what the reporter wanted and I had some time to prepare. I made a few notes, went for a walk through a nearby graveyard and talked to myself. I rehearsed just the way a television or radio reporter would.

When I returned to the office, I connected my tape recorder to the phone, called the reporter and began recording the interview, which lasted for a full hour. It filled both sides of a 60-minute audio cassette.

It was an invaluable learning experience because it put our media training methodology in perspective.

Early in our media training sessions, participants are exposed to brief, 30-second interviews where they're asked non-threatening questions such as, "Is there anything else you'd like to add?" The idea is to get them used to facing reporters, cameras, lights and microphones. They also learn the importance of using visual imagery to give more impact to their words and the value of eye-contact, body language, facial expressions and hand gestures.

In the afternoon, we simulate a wide range of media interviews, from one-on-ones to scrums and news conferences. Most last about five minutes. We can't simulate a one hour interview because it would take up too much of the training day — unless we are specifically coaching a client who knows she is about to face such an interview.

After my one hour encounter I realized that, as tough as our media training is, there's nothing we can do to make our simulations as bad as real life can be. This reaffirmed my contention that training should he harder than real life because you can't take all the skills you learned in practice into a real situation. The same is true in sports. You're not as good in a real boxing match as you were in training. The same is true in academic life. You're not as good in an oral defence of a thesis or research proposal as you are on paper or in the library.

At the end of the hour, the journalist had the best perspective I could put on the story. He knew that contracts with the federal government were subject to tender and competitive bidding. He knew that bills were issued in accordance with published rules and guidelines. He also knew that I regularly travelled to Asia for the Government of Hong Kong, or other local clients. The Canadian taxpayer got a very good price for sessions while I was in the region.

I felt I had done well, but still listened to the tape for any weaknesses. I found a few areas where I could have been stronger and others that the reporter didn't fully understand. I had one last chance to bolster my position. We had discussed a small, laminated wallet card that I give out to participants, which the reporter hadn't seen. I faxed him a copy and in the cover note included some additional information and clarifications.

But even now, at this late stage, I knew the reporter was free to write whatever he wanted and his newspaper was free to publish almost anything. I felt as though I had just lit a long fuse — without knowing what was at the other end.

Ten days later I found out I was not the focus of the story at all. It turned out the reporter had a juicier story than my billings and I was mentioned only peripherally. His story also reflected a dislike of media trainers who help their sources to do better in interviews. He had found someone trained by my competitor. He interviewed the journalist who had interviewed that client and the journalist said the interview would have gone better and he'd have had a better story if the guest had not been media trained!

Reporters usually advise people to simply be available and tell the truth. There are two problems with this: first, being available when you're not prepared is dangerous; second, the definition of truth is open to discussion. What if my wife asks me: "How do I look in this dress?"

If I answer, "Great," what is the truth that the statement speaks of? *Did I mean:*

"You're the nicest looking woman I've ever seen."
"That dress hides your extra pounds well."
"Looking at you in that dress excites me."
"We're going to be late for the play."
"You look exactly as you did 22 years ago."
"I still love you."
"I can't afford to buy you a new dress."

For me, truth occurs in a context. I think newsmakers need to know both the public policy and the journalistic contexts in which they are operating. That's what we do in media training.

I tell this story about my interview to illustrate the labour intensity of proper media relations. I spent about five hours dealing with that journalist. I was lucky in that he was really after something else and that I only appeared in a few innocuous quotes buried in the middle of his story. But it could have gone another way. Who knows what effect my research, rehearsal, calls to my competitor and lawyer, written communication and taping had on the finished product?

Most people wouldn't think of spending five hours getting ready for an interview. But I did — and I had the built-in advantage of being a reporter for 14 years and teaching media training for 10 years by that time. Yet, I still felt the need to prepare seriously and hope you will too.

Interview Techniques:
> Communication requires simplicity and clarity
> Quote the experts to augment your credibility
> Listen to the questions
> Be forthright and obliging

Avoid These Hazards:
> N>P (A negative is greater than a positive – avoid them)
> Lengthy explanations: deliver your SOCKO immediately
> Ambiguous questions: ask for clarification
> Assumptions and conjecture: deal with the realities
> No Comment: explain why it is inappropriate to answer questions
> Inducements to talk "off the record" or "on background." There's no uniform definition for these terms, even among journalists
> Bureaucratese, legalese, slang, double-talk
> Staring into the camera: speak to the questioner (except where the interviewer is in a different location, in which case the camera becomes the focus of your attention. This is sometimes referred to as a double ender or remote interview)
> Fidgeting, fussing, fiddling with pens or jewelry or gripping the chair: sit up straight, lean forward, be earnest. Swivel chairs may encourage you to fidget, so avoid them.

Make sure the reporter can reach you for additional information or clarification. Don't ask or expect to have any say in editing or reviewing the reporter's story before it's printed or broadcast. Should a story be published that is genuinely misleading, contact the reporter, then the editor, to ask for a correction.

Up to now we've used the term "interview" to broadly cover any conversation with reporters. But you only have to watch television, listen to radio and read newspapers to see there are in fact several different forms and types of interviews. While the general rules and concerns apply to all, each type of interview also has its own unique properties.

Print interviews for newspapers or magazine's won't be made public for hours and sometimes weeks and their contents are usually edited. Television and radio interviews may be live and unedited, or edited and broadcast later as part of a news report or feature item.

Let's take a closer look.

Print Interviews

Assuming they are pre-arranged these tend to be longer and more "in depth" than interviews for radio or television. Therefore it is necessary to have more detailed background for your SOCKOs, and more anecdotal material. This is an opportunity to expand upon and convey your message to the audience, but that doesn't mean you can ignore the rules on brevity and clarity.

Don't forget a print reporter is also part of your audience and capable of drawing his or her own conclusions about how you look and sound — and then reporting them. Just because there isn't a camera present to record you slouching in your chair doesn't mean the world won't find out about your apparent lack of interest in the subject under discussion. Reporters often review your demeanour, tone, gestures and body language as if you were on TV. They can make you look intransigent, silly or worse with descriptive phrases such as:
> "An obviously uncomfortable and unhappy Mr. Bloggins asserted . . . ."
> "Seemingly unconvinced of the merits of her own new policy, the CFO contended . . . ."

Even a print interview over the telephone can lead to your being described as "hesitant" or "unknowledgeable."

These may cast enormous doubt on your position and you must work hard to avoid such descriptions.

As with any kind of interview, the length and tone is usually decided by the interviewer. Even if there are no time constraints don't be surprised if the reporter interrupts your answers to make a comment, re-ask the same question or even change the focus.

Print interviews are useful for providing reporters with background and context. However, don't be lulled into a false sense of security. Reporters are looking for the unusual and will probe and prod until they find it. Make sure the background and context you provide are accompanied by appropriate SOCKOs.

Broadcast Interviews

Because they use your image and the sound of your voice, radio and television interviews allow for a more personal contact with the audience. On the other hand, a person listening or watching you at home can't interrupt you to say: "I'm sorry, I didn't quite catch that. Can you please repeat it?"

For all intents and purposes you have one chance, and once chance only, to say what you'd like to say in the way you'd like to say it.

Broadcast studios are expensive places to build and maintain and their use may be rationed among different departments and programs. If you agree to a studio interview, be on time and preferably a bit early. You may have all sorts of valid reasons for arriving 15 minutes late but if the studio was only available for 15 minutes you'll be out of luck. Worse, the producer and reporter — the people on whom you are relying to portray your enterprise in a good light — will have a reason to dislike you.

Arriving early also will give you an opportunity to familiarize yourself with the studio atmosphere so that you aren't intimidated by all the strange equipment. Naturally, you should also have some background on the person interviewing you or, at the least, the program for which you are being interviewed.

On radio, your voice is the only conveyance for your message. The people listening to you may be driving, cooking, gardening, jogging or working in the garage. What they take away from listening to you will depend on you vitality, strength, enthusiasm and confidence.

Conversational tones can be helpful in establishing your competence and confidence. But if you want to stress some points over others you will have to vary the pitch and tone of your voice. Occasional pauses and repetitions can also be effective.

In order to be able to use your voice to best advantage, you have to practise good bio-mechanics. You need to sit straight, on the edge of your chair, leaning slightly forward from the waist. This creates a straight line between your navel and your nose so that you can create an effective column of air on which to speak. You can also breathe in more air between phrases so that you can keep talking. Newscasters are taught to sit this way, why shouldn't you?

If you want to check whether you are sitting correctly, try to stand up without having to push up with your arms or shifting your feet. Sit towards the front of the chair with your feet flat on the floor. Now you should be able to flex the thigh muscles and stand straight up.

Remember: there are no visual aids in radio. Be careful about using complex numbers or phrases such as: "As you can see on this chart . . . ."

Many radio interviews are conducted by telephone and because this is such a familiar way for us to converse with others, there's always the chance of us letting down our guard. Don't. Never forget you are talking to a reporter. Assume you are being recorded, even if you're not.

A favourite trick of radio interviewers is the challenging silence. Just when you are expecting another question — there isn't one. Instead, there's an expectant silence inviting you to say more. Resist the temptation. Let the silence continue and you'll find the interviewer will eventually break it.

If the interview does not occur in a radio studio, it's entirely possible you'll find yourself talking to a complete stranger who is holding a microphone very close to your mouth. While this may seem intimidating, that's not the intent. Radio reporters want to get the cleanest and clearest audio they can and the best way of doing that is placing the microphone as close as possible to the source.

Some people have an overwhelming urge to seize and hold the microphone for themselves. This only causes friction with the reporter and should be avoided.

On television, your voice and your appearance are equally important. Both will influence the way you are judged by the audience.

Depending on the subject matter of the interview, your choice of dress and the setting for the interview may also be important. People tend to "dress up" to be on television. However wearing a formal business suit while sitting at a polished boardroom table won't help you explain why it is necessary to damage a small town's economy by closing down one of your manufacturing plants just before Christmas. Dress appropriately.

Even though television reporters prize spontaneity, don't be surprised if the interviewer decides to cut you off in mid-answer and say: "Let's begin again." It may be for technical reasons, or it may be that you look and sound up-tight and uncomfortable. It may annoy you, but stay focused on what you want to say.

TV Tips

> Ignore the camera. Indeed if you are in a studio there may be more than one camera and you won't know which one to look at! Keep your attention fixed on the host or interviewer.

> If standing, lean forward about five degrees and gesture with your palms open. Be engaged, not defensive. Don't rock on your feet. Use the same sitting posture described above for radio, but make some cosmetic concessions for TV. Cross legs at the ankles or knees and be ready to lean into the questioner for emphasis.

> If you are in a chair, sit up and slightly forward to let the audience know you are interested and fully engaged in the process.

> Exude vitality. Use both hands to gesture with palms at 45 degrees and elbows at 90 degrees. When the topic is grave, tone down the body language.

> Avoid sitting between two interviewers, or between two other guests,

since this will force you to constantly turn from one to the other during responses.

> If it is necessary to change your body position, do so slowly. Any sudden movements could actually take you out of the camera's view.

> Your part in a news item may be edited to less than 8 seconds. Be sure your SOCKOs are clear and concise.

> A talk show is more natural and conversational. You are there to inform and entertain the audience. The shorter the interview, the more concise the message must be.

> With two or more guests on a talk show, you may be fighting for air time. Many guests think that producers want them to compete. Is this the best venue for you?

At the conclusion of a television interview, be aware that the cameras and microphones may still be "hot" so be sure to maintain your professional appearance and posture until you are absolutely sure you are not still on camera, or until you have left the studio.

Broadcast interviews, whether conducted in studios or outside — on location — can have a different "look" and "feel" to them depending on the broadcasting organization's style, the facilities available, the type of program and time considerations. Here are some different formats and venues you may encounter:

Radio or TV "stand-up" interview: This nearly always takes place away from the studio. As the name implies you and the reporter stand face to face. For television, the camera is usually aimed at you over the reporter's shoulder. In some cases you may find the camera operator and reporter are one and the same. In this case you will usually be told where to look.

Radio or TV "sit-down" interview: The location may be your office, your home or any room with two chairs. Again, the TV camera is usually aimed at you over the reporter's shoulder. Some television programs like to place you, the guest, alongside the interviewer so a single camera can show both of you.

Very few non-studio interviews make use of more than one camera. So for editing reasons, you may be asked to stand or sit still after the interview while the camera takes shots of the reporter re-asking the questions, or nodding silently.

Radio studio or booth interview: Some radio studios are not much bigger than broom closets and, in an effort to keep the temperature down, lighting is kept to a minimum. If you are claustrophobic make your objections known before you are shoe-horned into one! Don't be intimidated by the wires, the professional looking microphones and headsets. If you are the only person being interviewed you won't have to wear a headset and the microphone will be turned on and off for you by the technician in the control room.

Radio call-in or talk show: This may involve other people in different locations and that means you will have to wear a headset to hear them. If you are the "expert" and people are calling in to ask you questions or challenge your views you will have no trouble knowing when to speak and when to keep silent. However if you are just one among "equals" you can't always rely on the host ensuring that you will have your say. Before the program begins, ask the host what the rules are. Some producers want a measured approach, others prefer a free-for-all.

TV Studio Interview:
There's no end of possibilities. Some news programs will place you next to or opposite a news anchor or host so you can be interviewed live during a newscast. Others will place you in an armchair behind a coffee table or on a stool at a counter-top. Unlike radio studios, TV studios are very bright places and they can be quite warm, particularly if you are required to wear make up.

TV Panel Discussion:
These generally involve a round-table format or a variation of one. Again, don't be afraid to ask the anchor/host what the rules are before the program starts. This is particularly true if you are a guest panelist with a bunch of regulars. They will know the ropes, you won't.

TV Remote, or "Double-Ender" Interview:
This is probably the most difficult type of interview you will encounter,

not because of the questions, but because of the technical format. In this case you will be interviewed standing up or sitting down, outside your plant gate or in your office or even in a remote studio. You will have to use a small earphone to hear questions posed by an interviewer who may be in another country, and aim your answers at the camera lens. It is difficult to maintain your focus under these conditions, but focus is vital to maintain your credibility.

News Conference:
This permits a large number of reporters and news outlets to question you at the same time. As such it is a compromise. Individual reporters know they won't be able to ask as many questions of you as they'd like, and you know you won't be able to have as much control over the questioning as you'd like. To work well, a news conference has to have a formal structure (See Page 108), otherwise it will degenerate into a free-for-all, or scrum.

The foregoing examples all require some sort of pre-arrangement between the parties. Reporters approach you, or your public affairs office, and request an interview. Then you agree on the type of interview, it's location etc. But you may also encounter the media unexpectedly, either because there's no time to formally request an interview (as in the case of an emergency), or because you have ignored repeated requests for interviews.

Scrums

A scrum is an unscheduled interview involving any number of reporters from any type of media and can take place at almost any venue where reporters and news makers come into contact. Do not be seen to be avoiding a scrum. On camera it will appear that you are being evasive.

Scrums can be unnerving as reporters and photographers jockey for position in crowded circumstances, so do remain calm, choosing the questions you prefer to answer. Don't look as if you are fearful of reports, or the scrum. If you are caught in one, you have to perform safely and professionally. Do not allow your answers to become rushed but try to keep them brief.

You can lessen reporters' enthusiasm for scrums if you schedule one-on-one interviews or news conferences. However, you still need to know the rules of the scrum:

1)   Have three or four messages or themes to deliver and repeat. Rehearse them out loud in advance.

2)   If there is little positive to be gained from answering questions, keep walking slowly, be pleasant, serious and keep repeating your position.

3)   If there is something to be gained-new information to get out, the record   to correct and you have several positive messages committed to mind-walk out to meet reporters, stop and deliver your messages. Use the SOCKO system: deal with the question then bridge to your message.

4)   Look the reporter in the eyes to acknowledge the question, answer the reporter while maintaining eye contact, then acknowledge another reporter in turn.

5)   For most situations, imagine your peripheral vision encompasses an area demarcated by a 45 degree angle emanating from your eyes. Don't turn your head beyond this angle, otherwise the camera in front of you will only get a shot of your ear.

6)   Stay cool. Don't get as excited as the reporters seem to be. Take a deep breath, think, then answer.

7)   Treat hecklers and other non-reporters like any other stimulus. Address hecklers' questions if reporters want you to. Tell hecklers you will meet with them to address their concerns.

8)   Once you feel you have delivered your message satisfactorily tell the reporters you have time for only two more questions. When those have been dealt with, say "thank you" in a clear, loud voice and begin moving to end the proceedings. Once you are moving, don't stop. If you have an assistant with you, he or she can announce the end of the encounter.

Ambush Interviews

These may occur if you refuse to grant a formal interview. Reporters may confront you in the street or in the car park and begin to question you in an excited and aggressive manner. It's more of a confrontation than an interview, one designed to show that reporters are diligently pursuing the facts.

Should you find yourself in this situation, try to appear cooperative and open with whatever information you may make available. It's easy to look guilty. Running, or even walking quickly to your car, hurrying to roll up car windows, struggling with car keys, trying to shut an office door quickly behind you will all make you look evasive, if not guilty. Remember that cameras and microphones may be aimed at you and your reactions will be on view. Be calm and state why it is not appropriate to discuss the matter in public.

If possible try to establish exactly what the reporter wants to know. Then ask for time to refer to your files and facts of the case, collect your thoughts and explain in detail why you are not free to disclose the information. Assure reporters that you will disclose it as soon as you are authorized to do so. If you get an opportunity deliver prepared, rehearsed SOCKOs.

A word about the closeness of media encounters: Unless you happen to be interviewed over the phone, or in a remote location, you will find that many media encounters are conducted at extremely close range. This may be for technical reasons or lack of space, or it may be because the encounter occurs in a very public and possibly noisy location and people want to hear what you are saying.

Most of us don't like others invading our personal space but if you are working with the media it is quite common. If it bothers you, try not to show it. Training and practice in these formats will lessen your nervousness and help you look, sound and be confident when the time comes.

Attitudes

An interview usually involves two people. They will have different agendas, expectations, characters and styles. Because of these differences they will almost certainly approach the encounter in different ways. They will have different a-t-t-i-t-u-d-e-s.

The Newsmakers' Attitude

I've recently been on a book tour and been through most of these formats in London, England, New York and many other major North American cities. I know very well what can go wrong in an interview, and I also know the tough questions I would have asked had I been interviewing someone who'd written the books in question. But, I never ran into unfair questions. The toughest questions were about what I charge and the ethics of advising and training people to be better news sources. I am now convinced that most spokespeople go into a media encounter with a far bigger chip on their shoulders than the reporter does.

Many encounters during my time as host and interviewer on a morning radio show illustrate the need to do homework, have all the facts, be responsive — and above all, remove that chip from your shoulder and leave it at the door.

One of the reasons for this attitude on the part of newsmakers has to do with rank. Their ego is involved and so is fear of the unknown. But the real issue is rank. Many newsmakers carry titles such as President or Vice President. They could also be doctors, lawyers or other professionals with long strings of letters after their names. I often remind newsmakers they aren't the Vice President of the newspaper they're visiting or the radio and TV stations they're touring.

Titles don't carry the same weight when they travel outside their own organizations.

The skills that make a person successful at work may mean little or nothing in the media hot seat. There, an ability to read a spread sheet, an expertise in law or engineering and undoubted management skills are often of less importance than body language and the ability to speak clearly and succinctly.

Before I started this company my job was Manager of Government Relations for a TV network. I had a budget of $5000 per year. My partner in New York, before he set out on his own, was Manager of Communication for Exxon and had a $60 million per year budget. Obviously the rank of Manager means quite different things in different companies. Media people notice that almost everyone in banks seem to be Vice Presidents, AVPs, EVPs or SVPs, so titles quickly lose their impact.

People with rank also get into the habit of assuming that others will follow their orders. The only thing that many senior executives have heard in the few weeks before they come in for coaching in The Centre is, "Yes, Bob," "You were right, Bob," "We'll get right on that, Bob," and so on. Their reflexes are not ready for "Why, Bob?" "Why on earth would you do it that way, Bob" or, "Nonsense, Bob!"

It can be tough for them at first, but if they stick with it and learn not to rely on their rank they will soon be well prepared for tough journalists and their questions.

The Reporters' Attitude

I earned an undeserved reputation as a tough, and even unfair, interviewer after an encounter with a spokesperson for a charity. Somebody came on my show wanting to publicize a dance to raise money to save an historic building. After we got through the pleasantries of time, place, costume, band and so on, I asked how much the charity had to raise to save the building. The spokesperson didn't know.

"Why do you ask," she asked. (I generally advise against asking questions of hosts, live, on air because it's the host's show and you may not like the answer you get).

"Why do I ask?" I exclaimed. "I ask because I think the people you are trying to sell tickets to might want to know if they are about to become involved in a hopeless lost cause or something that might do some good. If you tell me you have to raise $3000, I'm going to assume you have a good chance of success. But if you need to raise three million dollars, I can't see your doing that at this dance. And, I don't know how you run an event like this without knowing what your goal is." The rumour spread that if a church wanted to promote its annual fish fry, Bonner would try to expose the deadly effects of fried fish before the interview was over.

My morning radio show, like most others, was a mix of pre-taped material, pre-arranged live interviews and, sometimes, live interviews arranged "on-the-fly." One morning I was handed a piece of paper indicating that I was going to interview the Deputy Minister of Agriculture because he had just had a meeting with race track owners who were petitioning the Ministry for more financial subsidies to keep their race tracks afloat.

This didn't seem very interesting to me. I had no idea race tracks were subsidized, that they needed more money or that the Agriculture Ministry was involved. My scripted introduction and the interview that followed went like this:

Racetrack owners are worried about their finances. Fewer tourists are betting these days, so a group of owners has just had a meeting with the Deputy Minister of Agriculture to see if he can help with larger subsidies.

(AB)   Good morning, Deputy . . . .
(DM)   Good morning, Allan.
(AB)   How did your meeting with racetrack owners go?
(DM)   Full, frank, honest, open, timely, blah, blah, blah (or words to that effect)
(AB)   What are the next steps Deputy?
(DM)   Open door, open mind, working hand in hand, feedback, blah, blah, blah, (or words to that effect).

By this time we were about two minutes into a five minute interview and I was no more interested in the topic than when I began. To help me get a handle as to what this was all about I asked:

(AB)   Why do we allow betting at racetracks, Deputy?
(DM)   That's policy. (Only a Deputy Minister would think this tautology is an answer)
(AB)   But why is it policy?
(DM)   Well, it's long-standing policy. (Only a Deputy Minister would think this added something to his previous answer).
(AB)   Yes, but why is it long-standing policy?
(DM)   That's a policy question and you'll have to ask the Minister.

The Minister was not on my show that morning and I needed to get something of substance out of this guy before the next minute or so expired, if only to preserve my reputation with my listeners.

(AB)   Surely you can tell me something about this policy question, such as when it became policy or about the benefits to the tax payer because of this policy, or the options debated before it became policy. Can't you?

(DM)   No, why do you ask?

(AB)   Why do I ask? I ask because we put people in jail for betting at football games. We put people in jail for betting at baseball games and we don't allow betting at hockey games. But we do allow betting at race tracks! Not only do we allow betting at race tracks, but we're so keen on this activity that the government subsidizes it. Now I think the taxpayers listening to this program not only want to know what benefit this is to them, but they want to know that you, at least, know why you are doing it. That's why I ask! *(Asked with only the righteous indignation that a young journalist can muster. But I did envision his staff coming in each week helping to manipulate his hand as he signed checks, unaware and uncaring of what he was doing. Surely this couldn't be the case?).*

I ended the interview. No doubt this man still tells the story of the obnoxious interviewer who insisted on asking him a question that a Minister might rightly field. But my position is that, if you are a Deputy Minister responsible for a piece of public policy, the least you should know is its history, purpose, alternatives and outcomes. Whether it should be changed or whether it should have been enacted at all, is, indeed, a question for a Minister, but the rest should be in a competent briefing long before the interview takes place so the Deputy can field such procedural questions.

Here's one more personal experience that illustrates the need to be forthcoming and cooperative. Again, it was my morning show and I was handed a last minute introduction for a live interview that went something like this:

The agency that regulates telephone service, the CRTC, held a hearing in Xville (small town in Eastern Ontario) last night. The residents of Xville were demanding an upgrade of their equipment, which would give them faster and more reliable phone service. On the line is Joe Smith, Eastern Ontario Manager with the Bell Telephone.

(AB)   Good morning, Mr. Smith.

(JS)   Good morning, Allan.

(AB)   Mr. Smith, are the citizens of Xville going to get upgraded service?

(JS)   Well, that's up to the CRTC to decide; you'd have to ask them. I'm not prepared to discuss that.

(AB)   Yes, what did you think of their presentation. Did it have merit, hold water . . . did you see their point of view?

(JS)   Well, their presentation was to the CRTC, not to Bell, so I'm not prepared to discuss that.

(AB)   OK, let's say the CRTC decides in favour of Xville, how quickly could you get their service upgraded?

(JS)   That's a hypothetical question, so I'm not prepared to discuss it.

(AB)   Well, what on earth are you prepared to discuss this morning?

(JS)   That's about it. (I'm not kidding)

(AB)   Goodbye.

I was livid. I called the head of PR for the phone company to complain but he was in a meeting. I asked if he was the person in charge of media relations and when that was confirmed I said:

"Well, I'm a member of the media and I wish to have relations with him, so get him out of the meeting!"

When he came on the line and heard my story, all he could say was that Mr. Smith didn't usually handle media calls. That made me even angrier. Why would a major company designate a spokesperson who had no knowledge of the subject being discussed, nor even any interest in portraying his company in a good light?

Surely Mr. Smith could have said something about the complexities of changing telephone systems under a regulated monopoly (as it was then). He could also have said how enlightening it was to hear the views of customers and that if the CRTC approved their request, the company would give it prompt consideration.

I wasn't expecting him to commit the company to spending any money, but I did expect Mr. Smith, or any other designated spokesperson for that matter, to be able to say something intelligent.

The conversation ended with my feeling better for having blown off some steam and the PR VP having his worst fears about media people confirmed.

The point again is: do your homework. Anticipate questions. Have answers or reasons for not having answers.

Answering Questions

Q & A Pitfalls

I probably did about ten thousand interviews as a young broadcaster. I learned a lot in the editing room where I had to listen to the interviews several times each to check the length and flow. I also had to edit. When you edit, you listen for superfluous words. I heard how I sometimes didn't get an answer or was satisfied with an answer to a question I hadn't asked. I heard how some guests could succeed and others fail with the same content.

I realized that people have a tendency to construct their language in similar ways when they want to attack you or your ideas. There are only so many ways that can be used to cut the ground out from under a person — and it helps if you can identify them.

The Set-Up or False Premise

It's often couched in reasonable terms, but it is still false and must be dispelled politely and firmly. Don't nod your head to indicate you understand the question. It may look as you agree with the false premise.

The Either/Or Question

There is no reason for you to choose between unacceptable alternatives. You can answer, "neither," clarify your role, the subject matter you can speak about and move on to talk about your issues.

The Irrelevant Question

Perhaps the journalist had other things on her mind. Maybe the researcher got it wrong. Whatever the reason, you may have to deal with irrelevant questions. Be nice. Don't attack. Smoothly get on to your topic.

Sandbag/Blind Side

Without warning, the sandbag falls on your head, as in a cartoon. A short, tough question comes up, giving you little or no time to think. "You should resign" is an example. Well, one answer is, "No!" You can also give the reason why you shouldn't resign. Another approach is to use a "key word" from the question to help construct a bridge to your answer. "What I should do is . . . ."

The Empty Chair

An old visual trick in television used to be to put an empty chair on a stage when a political debate was being held if one of the candidates refused to attend. Producers might even put the candidate's name on the chair to drive home the fact he didn't show up. This is considered unethical now, but a version remains. Reporters may dig up an old study, a fact, a quote from an expert or other bit of information to surprise you on air.

Don't talk about things you don't know about. Tell the reporter you are unfamiliar with the quote, but will study it, in context, and provide a reaction later. You can also point out, politely, that if you had been given notice that the reporter wanted a reaction to that fact, you would have looked into it and provided one.

Rambling/Historical/Multiple Questions

You may be in mid-interview when the reporter begins to review the history of a policy, academic studies, landmark court decisions and quotes from other newsmakers of the past. The reporter may be showing off, or may just be lost. Cherry pick an aspect of the question you want to deal with and run with it. This works in scrums and news conferences too, when you are getting several reporters talking at once. Pick one and answer. Then move on to the next. Don't try to memorize all the questions or aspects of questions.

Flip-Flop

This is the reporter's term for a change of policy. You need to explain that while circumstances have changed, necessitating a change in tactics and actions, your overall approach and determination to do the right thing has not changed.

The Unfocused Question

Many journalists don't feel the need to formulate a question. They throw out a fact, statistic or quote and sit back and wait for a reaction rather than an answer. Worse yet, they may just blurt out, "Really," "Seriously?" "Come on," or another exclamation.

Increase your own energy level, find a key word and re-state your case: "Yes, really. That's what we're going to do and I know it'll work."

What If?

Don't speculate. Be safe. Discuss only what you know for sure, not something hypothetical.

Challenging Silence or Pregnant Pause

Most of us feel uncomfortable with silence in the middle of a discussion or interview and try to fill the gap. We say something, even though there may be no reason to fill the void. This is how we make gaffes.

Don't ramble on. An interview is not a cocktail party or blind date. Use a SOCKO to reinforce your position, or simply wait for the questioning to resume.

No Comment

This tells reporters that you have something to hide. They'll keep probing!

There may be several reasons for you not to discuss something in public. You may be ignorant of the issue; there could be judicial, medical, ethical and other reasons that prevent you from talking. Explain the reasons. Your audience may not like your reasons, but they'll be less likely to question your motives.

One of the main reasons people give for not speaking about an issue is that "it's before the courts." Most questioners will accept this, even though it's not a valid reason for not speaking. You want to succeed in court, and in the court of public opinion!

Off the Record

There's no good definition of what this means. It's the same with "on background", "deep background" or "not for attribution." They can mean different things to different people in different parts of the world.

If you don't want to be quoted on a particular issue, don't talk about it. The only thing that's off the record is what you didn't say.

Accusation/Negative

Remember that "N" is always greater than "P" (N>P). Negatives carry greater weight than positives, so steer clear of them. By repeating the negative, your are simply bringing it to the attention of people who may not have heard that perspective before. So be positive.

Bridging the Gap Between Questions and Answers

There are many ways of responding to a question without having to blurt out something you'd rather not say.

Don't avoid questions from journalists. In fact the "technique" you should use most often is a Clear Question/Direct Answer. This shows that you've done your homework and you know your subject.

But reporters need more than "yes" or "no," "May 15th," "16 tonnes" or whatever. Add a SOCKO. Every question is an opportunity for you to say something positive about yourself, your organization or your concerns and issues.

Key Wording

Reporters may use one of your own words to move the discussion down a new track. You can do this, too. Take a key word from the question and use it as a semantic bridge to get to what you want to talk about.

Mirroring

Here, you can take the opposite approach. If reporters want to focus on problems, you can talk about solutions. Problems and solutions are closely linked and the change of focus seems natural.

Another type of mirroring reflects the mood and words of the questioner: "I can see you are frustrated and you'd like more answers, and I'm going to try to get them for you," and so on.

Parallel Construction

If reporters want information on fees or cost, you may prefer to talk about results or value. Fees and results and cost and value are close enough in concept that they can be used in parallel.

If the issues or concepts are too far apart (i.e. the question is about fees but you wish to talk about the qualifications of those charging the fees) you will have to find a semantic bridge or use another technique to bring the concepts closer together.

Concessions

These must be very small and designed to help you make a larger point. An accusation about your competence must not lead to a concession about how you wish you were smarter. All you need to concede is that we all make mistakes occasionally and the trick is to learn from them.

Newsmakers often overdo concessions. Don't say, "I see your point," if you don't want to be quoted as agreeing with the point. If you are being accused of doing something bad in the past, but you have no knowledge of it, don't say, "Maybe no one knew any better." That's how you'll be quoted and no one will see the other five times you said other things. You may also be paraphrased as conceding that your organization does not have a history of knowing right from wrong."

Concessions must be small and create a bridge to the questioner: "No one is perfect, but here's what we're trying to do now."

Cherry Picking

This is the solution to multiple questions from either one reporter or a group of reporters in a news conference or scrum. Be selective and focus on one aspect about which you are knowledgeable and comfortable.

> Example: "How can you explain this disaster? Why did it happen and what are you doing to do about it?"
Solution: "We're going to ensure that people get to shelters quickly." *(Cherry pick; direct answer)*

Better: "We're trying to analyze those questions but our main goal right now is getting people into shelters." *(Small concession, refocus)*

Better still: "No one knows all those answers but we may find out soon. We'll keep you posted, but for now we're focusing on getting people into shelters." *(Direct answer precluding a follow up, small concession, refocus)*

Refocusing

This involves looking at an issue from a different perspective. Don't accept the reporter's point of view if it's damaging to you—refocus!

> Example: "Why did you waste money on this . . . ?"

Solution: "My main focus right now is . . . ." *(refocus, parallel construction)*

Better: "Finances are important but my main focus right now is . . . ."*(concession, dignify, refocus)*

Better still: "Finances are important and we'll provide an accounting when we can, but right now me must stay focused on . . . ."

Telescoping

As it's name implies this helps you refocus on the big picture. Instead of talking about the needs of one community, you can stress the needs of a country or continent.

> Example: "Why did you waste money on this . . . ?"

Solution: "Our overall financial picture is very strong." *(Obtuse, ignoring of the question)*

Better: "We're not happy about this one area, but overall our financial picture is very strong." *(Concession, telescope or refocus)*

Better still: "Not all of our decisions are perfect. However, the vast majority are excellent and that's why our overall financial picture is very strong." *(Concession, telescope, bridge)*

Microscoping

This is the opposite. The focus is on the smaller, more personal picture. One family's needs may be easier to understand than an entire population's.

> Example: "Why did you waste money on this . . . ?"

Solution: "Not all of our decisions are perfect, but the vast majority are excellent. This makes our overall financial picture sound. Look at what we've been done for our oldest victim . . . ." *(concession, telescope, bridge and microscope)*

Flagging

The issues or concerns that you want to focus on may be completely different from those the reporter wants to raise. If you don't "flag" yours, both in the pre-interview with the producer and on air, on mic or on the record with the reporter, they may be ignored.

> Example: "Why did you waste money on this . . . ?"

Solution: "Do you mind if we focus on the victims for a moment . . . ?"

Better: "I'd like to deal with that, but first I want to . . . ."

Better still: "We'll have the answer to that in due course, but the most important thing right now is . . . ."

Like most skills these techniques will require practice. Here are some phrases to get you going. Develop your own and practise them:

Mirroring, Refocusing & Flagging
> The real issue here is . . .
> I'd like to emphasize . . .
> Let me begin with . . .
> I'd like to focus on . . .

Cherry Picking
> The most important point you raise is . . .
> Our main concern now is . . .
> Your questions raises the important issue of . . .
> Your question is important but right now we must focus on . . .

Small Concessions
> Perhaps, but we're working on . . .

> That may be part of the reason we are . . .
> I understand your concerns . . .
> I can see how someone might get that impression . . .

Telescoping
> All our customers are treated with respect . . .
> Everyone will benefit in several ways . . .
> Our history in this area is . . .

Microscoping
> One case where this did work was . . .
> Ms. Smith benefited from this plan . . .
> I was meeting with one affected person who said . . .

Remember: Anything that allows you to move from the reporter's agenda to your own is "a bridge."

Answering Questions by Not Answering Them

Generally speaking, it is always better to answer questions than to avoid them. But you may not have all the information, your knowledge may be incomplete or there may be legal or other restrictions. It is possible to not answer without damaging your credibility.

One of the main pitfalls to avoid is begging the question. This is an often misused term to mean causing one to ask another question. This could loosely be termed a version of begging the question, but the official definition involves tautology. A tautology is a response that purports to be an answer, but really only contains the content of the question. Consider this exchange:

Reporter: "Why should people support you?"
Newsmaker: "I'm trustworthy."
Reporter: "How would the electorate know that?"
Newsmaker: "Because I'm honest."

This is a tautology, and officially begs the question. The reporter has asked for evidence of trustworthiness and instead of an answer has been given a synonym. Being trustworthy is being honest and vice versa.

The vast majority of journalists ask follow-up questions to something they've just heard. If you don't answer the question or try to dodge it you can be sure you'll be asked the same question in a different way and possibly more challenging questions as well.

Even if you can't directly answer a question, there are good and bad ways to do so. Here are some options (in ascending order of credibility).

1. *Silence* (ignore both the question and questioner)
2. *By-passing* (a psychological term, meaning to play dumb)

> Example: "Why did you waste money on this . . . ?"

Solution: "You know, we are really very careful with scarce public funds . . . ." Richard Nixon's, "I'm glad you asked me that question" is a version of by-passing. Nobody thought he was glad.

3. *Resistance*

> Example: "Why did you waste money on this . . . ?"

Solution: "I can't discuss that now."

Better: "I can't discuss that right now while our board committee is reviewing it."

Or: "I've only just arrived and I don't have all the facts."

4. *Attack (Negative Resistance)*

> Example: "Why did you waste money on this . . . ?"

Solution: "That's not the question. You should be asking about the victims. I'm shocked you can be so shallow."

Few people can get away with attacking journalists. Margaret Thatcher could, as could Pierre Trudeau. But you probably cannot.

Attacking the motives or highlighting the failings of a questioner is a transparent technique used by people who are unprepared to answer tough questions. It is no substitute for a positive answer outlining your policy, goals or beliefs.

5. Parallel Response

> Example: "Why did you waste money on this . . . ?"

Solution: "Victims need our attention the most right now . . . ." (Refocus from money to victims. This answer also offers some hope that the journalist might get more information about money at a later date, after victims have been looked after)

It should be obvious that use of a phrase to dignify the question makes it easier to divert attention away from money and towards victims. The response will appear to be more directly related and so will have more impact.

Some examples:

> "That's a good question . . . ." (trite and obvious).
> "There are a number of important questions we must deal with . . . ."
> "Money is important, but not as important right now as the victims . . . ."
> "We're working to get that answer . . . ."

What follows are examples of some of pitfalls and traps listed above matched with techniques to help you deal with them. Notice that I sometimes suggest using two techniques to deal with the same problem. This is like a slap shot in hockey where the power is derived from both the forward motion of the lower hand and the backward pull of the upper hand. Two hands are better than one, and, semantically, two techniques are often better than one.

The Set-Up

> Example: "Considering the low regard people have for this product anyway."

Solution: "I think what a lot of people agree on is that this product does the following . . . ." *(Refocusing)*

The Either/Or question

> Example: "Either you're naive or being paid to lie . . . ."

Solution: "Neither . . . ." *(Direct answer)*

Better: "Neither, my main role is . . . ." *(Direct answer & bridge)*

Better still: "My main role is . . ." *(Refocus & a parallel bridge)*

Even better: "Actually, my main accomplishment since joining this company has been . . . ." *(Instead of attacking the questioner, refocus on your accomplishments. The word actually is a soft refocus)*

The Irrelevant Question

> Example: "Why are grain prices so high?"

Solution: "Our main work in agriculture is the production of tractor parts." *(Parallel Refocus)*

Better: "Grain prices are important to many of our customers but I don't have any insight into that topic. My area of responsibility is tractor parts." *(Dignify the question, delegate to others, refocus)*

Better still: "While grain prices are an important issue, we manufacture tractor parts. However, one of our economists may have some data on that and I'd be happy to refer you to her." *(Dignify the question, harder delegation to others, refocus)*

Even Better: "We'd all like to know the answer to that because grain prices can have an impact on our business. We make tractor parts and our economists keep a close eye on agricultural prices. They may have some answers. If they do, I'll be happy to refer you to them. Meanwhile, I can tell you how our tractor parts help farmers keep their costs down." *(Dignify the question, even harder delegation to others at a later date, refocus, bridge)*

Don't get carried away! You don't want long answers, but the example above shows you the variety of techniques available.

Sandbag

> Example: "You're incompetent . . . ."

Solution: "No I'm not . . . ." *(Direct answer, but negative and confrontational)*

Better: "The most competent thing to do right now is . . . ." *(Key word or concept, bridge)*

Better still: "The glitch we ran into is . . . ." *(Key concept, refocus, bridge)*

Even better: "We have a highly competent team of . . . ." *(Key concept, mirrored, bridge)*

The Empty Chair

> Example: "I have a copy of the Smith report which proves . . . ."

Solution: "I haven't seen it." *(An answer, and true, but too short not forthcoming or helpful)*

Better: "I haven't seen that report. I'd be happy to give you an opinion when I've read it. What I can tell you on that topic is . . . ." *(Admission, which is a direct answer, offer, bridge)*

Better still: "I haven't seen that report. I'm sure some of our researchers

have and I'd be happy to refer you to them. What I can tell you is . . . ."
(Admission, stronger offer and rationale, bridge)

Revisionist History/Multiple Question

> Example: "How did this happen? Why did it happen? What are you going to do about the victims?"

Solution: "We're setting up shelters for victims right now . . . ." *(Cherry pick one question)*

Better: "We're working on some of those questions right now, but our most important goal is to get shelters set up for victims." *(Dignify, direct answer, bridge)*

Flip-Flop

> Example: "You said shelters were the most important goal. Now you say it's hiring insurance investigators. Why have you changed your mind?"

Solution: "Our goal is always the welfare of victims. Now we find the best thing for them is getting their insurance claims settled." *(Consistency, bridge)*

The Unfocused Question

> Example: "Seriously?" "Oh come on!" "Really?"

Solution: "Yes." *(Direct answer)*

Better: "Yes, really. That's what we're going to do and I know it'll work." *(Direct answer, key word, bridge to efficacy)*

What If?

> Example: "What if victims' claims are turned down?"

Solution: "The real issue here is getting those insurance people working." *(Refocus, parallel bridge)*

Better: "We don't want anyone to suffer. We'll monitor those claims to see if the victims are getting the help they need. Right now we want to get the insurance people working." *(Empathy, action, refocus)*

Challenging Silence or Pregnant Pause

Solution: "Another point that might be helpful right now is . . . ." *(Refocus)*

No Comment

> Example: "Haven't you paid damage settlements in the past?"

Solution: "Each case is different and I don't think it would be productive to compare one with another. I'd be happy to discuss it in more detail when all the facts are in."

Off the Record

> Example: "Off the record, what's the real story?"

Solution: "There's only one issue for us right now and that's the victims' welfare." *(Flagging)*

Chapter 7   The How-To

Organizations, institutions and companies that find themselves of inter-est to the media (whether they welcome that interest or not) may find they have to deal with large numbers of newspeople under a variety of circumstances. This can pose a considerable challenge to those who have little or no experience in dealing with the media.

Newspeople often seem demanding and pushy. They can be — even when you've invited them to your premises to hear your story and pro-vided them with coffee and donuts to make them comfortable. You don't have to like them. The only things that count are your professionalism in dealing with them and expertise in telling your story.

This is where you learn to become professional in dealing with the media en mass.

Organizing and Managing a News Conference

Apart from those involving disasters, crises and emergencies, news con-ferences are stage-managed events. A news conference can be a some-what cumbersome way of dealing with reporters, but it's used when there are too many requests for interviews or not enough time to sched-ule them.

We're often asked to rehearse spokespeople for a news conference that clients have scheduled for themselves or that have been arranged for them by a public relations agency. Often we find there's little or no rea-son to hold one, but the client wants to raise his or her public profile and the PR company is selling a service.

Don't call a news conference unless there's reason to believe the media will be interested in what you have to say, or unless it's in response to requests from the media. Nobody enjoys wasting time and that includes reporters and their editors.

Remember, a news conference won't satisfy everyone's needs.

Indeed, if it's poorly planned it may not meet anyone's needs, including yours. So before you go to the expense and trouble of a news conference, make sure one is needed.

Remember also that a news conference can bring added pressure, friction and a unique group dynamic. There is more of a chance that reporters will be probing, challenging and competitive.

There are four phases to effective news conference management:

1) Planning
2) Preparing
3) Managing the News Conference
4) Mingling (follow-up)

Planning

A complex event such as a news conference needs to be planned. Much can be done well ahead of time. Filling out a Media Advisory Form (See Appendix 3, Figure 3.4) and allowing a few minutes for thought and rehearsal can be of enormous benefit.

Meeting others' needs and deadlines is vital for effective communication. A news conference which is held just after the daily deadline of a newspaper is of little use to that paper. Ten minutes past the deadline is much the same as 23 hours past the deadline. There also needs to be sufficient time between the end of the news conference and the reporter's deadlines to allow for writing, editing, production (TV) and so on. Remote locations dictate longer times for such activities.

Generally, television requires the greatest lead time before broadcast, followed by print media, then radio. Unless an event involves death, spectacular news or a different time zone, its announcement should be timed with these needs in mind. Today's television crews and their equipment are highly mobile. This allows TV news to cover events much closer to deadline, or even live. Even so, barring special circumstance a news conference should end before 4:30 p.m.

The location of the event will be determined by circumstances. In an emergency or other unplanned occurrence, news conferences can be held almost anywhere. Large companies or organizations may have suitable space "in-house." Others will prefer to use hotel reception rooms or other facilities.

In non-crisis situations, reporters may be given a few days notice of a planned news conference by way of a media advisory. Where the news is negative there won't be much time. Reporters will show up and demand information and access to a spokesperson.

Once you have decided the subject matter warrants a formal news conference (assuming this is an option, not an emergency, and you have sufficient time) there are a number of things you can do:

> Find out the needs of the various media in your area regarding deadlines and if they have specialized reporters interested in the subject (organizations with public affairs/communications departments should already have this information).
> Arrange suitable training for potential moderators, technical experts and spokespeople.
> Prepare and update background material.
> Choose the location and ensure that someone is given the responsibility to ensure that all the human and physical assets are in place. The physical set up of the room is dealt with in the section following on *Preparation*.

Preparation

This is probably the most crucial factor in determining the success or failure of the undertaking. Even under the most intense pressure of a catastrophic emergency, some preparation — no matter how limited because of time constraints — will pay off.

What follows is a detailed road-map for use when the conditions are ideal. Cutting corners may be necessary because of specific conditions, but the more elements you can use the better off you'll be.

The News Conference Room

A news conference room should be laid out as indicated in the following diagram. Reporters should be greeted with an unobtrusive method of ensuring that they have a legitimate reason for being there and that their credentials are in order. Realistically, however, the media and public are unlikely to accept the barring of affected citizens from a quasi-public event such as a news conference. Among the best that can be hoped for is to obtain advance warning that third parties will be in attendance.

Reporters should pass through a progressively more stringent screening process. Outside the entrance of the briefing room should be a table with background materials followed by a security table for checking credentials, followed by a table at which each reporter signs in.

At the back of the room, a small platform or riser will be the most efficient place to locate television cameras. This will provide a clear shot over the audience to the front of the room. The cameras will also need a

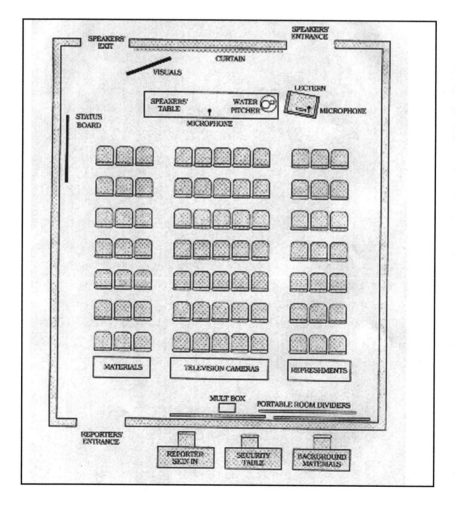

feed from the audio pool system.

A table with light refreshments and a table for materials may be placed at the back. The chairs should be laid out in theatre style with a wide aisle in the middle and on each side.

Where necessary, speakers may have to refer to Status Boards and/or Media Updates (see Appendix 3, Figure 3.9 and 3.10), maps, charts or other visual aids. The information table should contain the latest background material, news releases, bios, fact sheets and so on.

Room dividers are used in case few media people show up. The dividers are used to cut off corners or otherwise make the room smaller. Empty chairs can be stacked or removed.

The speakers' table should have a floor length cloth covering. Speakers should use pool microphones and be seated in front of a mid-blue curtain material and or an appropriate logo, slogan or product facsimile. There should be a rear entrance and exit so speakers can avoid scrums.

A P.A. system should be used for groups of 30 or more only. In order to gauge the correct room size, estimate the number of people expected and add 20%. The extra 20% is for cameras and equipment, and to account for the fact that hotels often overestimate the number of people who can comfortably fit into a room. Just be wary of a room that looks half empty if the news people don't show up.

A variety of outside resources must be available quickly in the case of breaking news or an incident (see Appendix 3, Figure 3.11). These should be updated annually to ensure that briefing rooms, audio-visual equipment, food and outside consultants are known and available.

A sample list of essential equipment (Appendix 3, Figure 3.6) should also be regularly reviewed and updated.

The appropriate site manager or communications manager should pre-assign some of the tasks of ensuring that the organization or location is ready to conduct a news conference. (See Appendix 3, Figure 3.7). This checklist must be regularly reviewed, updated and tested by locations such as regional offices or plants.

Dressing Rooms

A small room close to the news conference location should be reserved as a holding room for spokespeople. The room should have easy chairs and a full-length mirror. Before spokespeople leave for the news conference, someone should examine them discreetly but carefully to ensure they are presentable. Aim to have spokespeople in this room ten minutes before the news conference to allow them time to rehearse and compose themselves, and ten minutes afterwards to decompress.

News conferences should not be delayed because all these physical assets are not immediately in place. The most important aspect of any communication with reporters is the accuracy, timeliness and newsworthiness of the information conveyed. The news conference room can be upgraded as time goes on.

When a news conference is planned during an on going event, whether good news or bad, you may have only five minutes to "round up" all reporters on site. It is your responsibility to get them into the conference room — not their responsibility to know you have called a news conference. Depending on the site, you may find reporters using a phone, eating, shooting video outside or talking to sources. Find them!

Rehearsal

All spokespeople must be rehearsed on the type of questions that the media are liable to ask. The questions must be tough and realistic or the spokespeople will be lulled into a false sense of security. However, they must not be scared to the point of being too nervous to do a good job.

Spokespeople must be provided with a short analysis of the issues they may face and relevant information on the political district (if from out of the area), history of media and public interest in the organization and type of event. Someone from the organization must circulate among reporters before the conference and determine their level and areas of interest. This person can then use the sheet "journalistic questions" to help prepare the spokesperson (See Appendix 3, Figure. 3.5)

Participants must also be thoroughly briefed on the sequence of events planned for the news conference and the role of the moderator in directing the questions, handling difficult situations etc. No matter how senior the spokesperson is in an organization, it will serve no purpose for that person to be seen to be overruling or disagreeing with the efforts of the moderator to keep events proceeding smoothly.

Dress

Spokespeople should dress appropriately. Avoid seersucker, checkered suits, or fabrics with small repetitive patterns. In close up shots the lines in the suit will distort the video and create a distracting rainbow effect on the screen called "video crawl." Bracelets and any more than two rings should be removed. Women should wear longer hemlines and higher necklines and remove excessive necklaces and/or dangling earrings. Men in business suits need long, executive socks and shirts with larger neck sizes to avoid looking or sounding constricted.

Don't turn down any help if you're running a big event. First, you will need it. Second, it's good professional development for junior members of your staff. But use a checklist, so each person knows what to do and takes some of the pressure off you (See Appendix 3, Figure 3.8).

News Conference Countdown

A hypothetical ideal "time line" leading up to a news conference might be as follows:

60 minutes
Physical set-up is checked. Audience seating is positioned, risers for cameras set-up and the back-drop is put in place.

60 minutes
Television lighting of the set begins.

50 minutes
News conference set is complete. Graphics, name plates and support material are positioned.

40 minutes
P.A. system and audio pool feed systems are checked out. Lighting is

completed and checked for shadows.

40 minutes
Refreshments, media kits, background data and copies of speeches are put out.

20 minutes
Cold water (no ice) and glasses put on the head table.

5 minutes to 30 minutes
Media begin arriving and register for the news conference.

15 minutes to 5 minutes
Feed tone over the audio pool at 0 db, but not the P.A. system, so the radio reporters and television crews can calibrate their equipment (outside audio/visual company may be required).

Start
News conference starts.

Managing the News Conference

If you agree to a news conference at a press club or parliamentary press gallery, a senior member of that institution may act as moderator. If you arrange your own event, your organization's public affairs representative may be assigned to moderate.

Travelling delegations should be mindful of local customs. Many times an "availability" where the visiting dignitary agrees to linger after a speech or join the press table for a few questions will suffice. An availability can also mean making the newsmaker available in a hotel meeting room or other suitable location for an afternoon.

Before a formal news conference starts, the person chairing or acting as moderator should come to the lectern, introduce himself or herself and lay out the ground rules. The key for all participants is to be polite but firm and maintain the agenda.

Checklist for Moderators
> Brief spokespeople on local issues.
> Ask rehearsal questions with other public affairs staff.
> Go over each spokesperson's checklist.
> Check each spokesperson's attire and grooming.
> Provide pens, paper, water or other necessities to spokespeople.
> Insist on a minimum of ten minutes of quiet time before and after news conference.

Rules for Moderator
> Thank the media for showing up and introduce yourself.
> Announce any changes to previously arranged schedules, timings or facts.
> Both the moderator and officials should expect tough, even abrasive-sounding questions. They should focus on their answers and messages, and not get flustered.
> Announce if there is going to be an opening statement and explain other procedural matters.
> Identify by name and title the officials making statements. Indicate where their biographies and any other printed background and fact sheets can be picked up.
> State the length of time scheduled for questions and stick to it.
> Identify the technical experts who will be available for individual interviews after the news conference.
> Ask the media to identify themselves before asking questions.
> The moderator then calls for the spokespeople/experts to walk in and take their seats at their name cards.
> The moderator then calls for the opening statement.
> After the opening statement, the moderator calls for questions.
> Stipulate that one question and one follow up will be taken per reporter until everyone has had an opportunity to ask questions (time permitting).

Checklist for Spokespeople
> Use quiet room for 10 minutes before and after conference.
> Practise statements out loud at least three times. Practise responses to any tough questions you expect.

> List three or four simple messages or themes to which you wish to return regardless of the questions asked.
> Don't try to run the news conference-defer to the moderator.
> Don't argue with reporters.
> Stick to your areas of expertise!
> If you don't know, say so. Offer to find out and get back to the reporter as soon as possible. Then be sure you do!
> Keep your answers short and to the point.
> Be professional.
> If you don't want to see or hear it reported, don't say it!

During the News Conference

1) After statements have been made the moderator takes over again. Remind the media of how long the question period is and select the first reporter. (Some formats have reporters direct questions through the moderator for greater control).

2) If tension begins to build between the media and the spokesperson, the moderator must attempt to diffuse the situation.

3) About two minutes before the question period ends, the moderator should announce that there is time for two more questions.

4) After the time for questions has expired, the moderator will end the news conference by thanking the media for coming out. If it is part of the plan to offer technical spokepeople for individual interviews (a good idea!) the moderator will introduce them now. This will give time for the previous spokespersons to leave gracefully if they cannot remain.

5) The presentation can be enhanced by using maps, products, charts, aerial photographs, graphs or other usuals. This support material must be designed for use on television. Avoid too much detail and do not cover it with plastic because this will making photography difficult. The person referring to this support material must use a "lavaliere" microphone (clip on mike) around the neck and linked to the audio pool feed

system. Otherwise, the media will not be able to record the comments.

Tough Questions/Situations

Repetitive questions or lines of questioning which return to a controversial theme should be expected.

Arguing with reporters or walking out are not options. Only the moderator should interrupt a line of questioning or cut off one reporter and recognize another. The spokesperson should sit quietly and appear neutral should the moderator have to step in. It will serve no purpose for the speaker to overrule or argue with the moderator. However, the moderator should intervene only after one reporter has asked the same question at least three times, or if two or more reporters "gang up" to ask similar questions five times.

When that happens the moderator may:

1)   Indicate that the question has been answered "x" times to the best of the organization's ability, given the facts at hand.

2)   Point out that technical experts will be available later.

3)   Indicate that you have to be fair. Other reporters must be allowed to ask questions. Tell any persistent questioners that they will get another turn later.

4)   Promise to provide written material that may clarify the issue later.

5)   End the question period early. This should only be done as a last resort and in exceptional circumstances.

If the public or third party interest groups attempt to intervene, be polite and receptive. Here again, you or the moderator have some options:

1)   Indicate a public meeting is or will soon be scheduled.

2)   Offer to meet the questioner after the news conference.

3)   Point out a news conference is meant for reporters but if they don't object to giving up their time to questions from the public, you will cooperate. Let the reporters decide.

Depending on local circumstances it may be quite impractical to try to bar members of the public from attending a news conference. Many activists hold valid press credentials for periodicals or specialty publications. Moreover, if you get into an altercation with activists, that itself may become the news event covered by the reporters attending your news conference! The best strategy is to be prepared for tough questions from anybody.

Mingling (Follow-Up)

The end of news conferences is often a time for reporters to mingle with newsmakers and obtain clarification and additional background information. Unless the speaker is an extremely senior person with pressing business known to reporters, all organization officials should be encouraged to mingle after news conferences.

Some of the most important work surrounding a news conference takes place after it has finished. This is something widely recognized by politicians and other high profile people. It's the time their communication professionals go to work to try to "spin" the results favourably.

Even if your news conference doesn't seem to be the kind of event the requires spinning, the feedback you can get from reporters at this time will be a first indication of how you and your organization's message has been received.

Reporters may need:
>   Clarification
>   Spelling of names and titles
>   Spelling and definitions of technical terms
>   Still photographs
>   One-on-one interviews at a later time

> Reaction shots or cover footage of them with spokespeople

The moderator and other public affairs representatives should:
> Introduce themselves to individual reporters
> Ask if they have what they need to do a complete and thorough story
> Follow up on earlier questions or comments
> Reinforce the main messages of the spokesperson
> Try to detect the level and nature of interest
> Determine if additional action is needed to correct errors of omission or commission, or any misunderstandings

Reporter Pools & Photo Opportunities

You may also encounter the need to handle groups of news people simultaneously outside the confines of news conferences, whether formal or informal. These can be challenging experiences for management and staff who are not used to dealing with the demands of newspeople for instant access and information.

Individual reporters may be prepared to go through normal channels, submitting their requests for interviews and/or pictures and waiting at the reception desk or plant gate for a spokesperson to appear. But a pack of news hounds competing for a story will not be so accommodating.

Among the first things a group of reporters will request during their coverage of an event, product launch at a plant or trip to a new facility will be a visit to the site, conference room, ceremony or other newsworthy venues. Within reason these requests should be agreed to. In fact, it is beneficial to be in a position to offer press tours of such venues in advance of their request.

The philosophy behind this strategy is one of co-operativeness and the simple reality that reporters will do everything in their power to gain access to these venues regardless of the position of the authorities.

If reporters are visiting your site for an extended period of time, or if it's a bad news story and they're "camped out" at your site, information opportunities should be regularly scheduled and publicized on a

118 / ALLAN BONNER

flip chart or hand-delivered notes (See Appendix 3, Figure 3.13).

Reporter pools are a vital tool in the case of difficult-to-access sites, or where the number of reporters requesting access is too large to handle. A pool is a small representative group of reporters and photographers who obtain access to a site and then "pool" their information with their colleagues.

This system provides numerous advantages to managers:

> It eases security concerns
> It limits the spread of misinformation and rumours
> It reduces competition among journalists
> It demonstrates the event is being managed in a professional way

Get the journalists present to select a small group to visit the venue in question. It should include a newspaper reporter, a wire service reporter, radio and television reporters, a camera crew and a still photographer. Don't ignore language and cultural differences.

Pools may also present special security and legal challenges. In addition to the advice provided by legal counsel, you need to conduct accreditation checks, draw up indemnification agreements and offer safety briefings and the use of safety equipment where appropriate.

Photo opportunities are designed to provide the news media with the visual elements for their stories and items.

As you may remember from the diagram, "A Reporter's Building Blocks," (See Page 50) voice overs (narration) and visuals are an integral part of television news. If an organization denies media access to an incident, portion of the facility or some people within the facility, the reporter may simply expand his or her own commentary at the beginning and end, the time allotted to the third party experts and/or the time allotted to angry public reaction. The only purpose this will serve is to present the organization with a much tougher challenge.

Generally, photo opportunities are neutral or positive for the organization. They do not contain the confrontational elements of news conferences or interviews . Much of what reporters shoot will appear mundane to you (logos, building exteriors, equipment, people). Reporters will always look for movement, colour and the unusual. A confrontation, especially with the press, will make the most exciting visual possible and is to be avoided at all costs.

Even if reporters do not ask for a photo opportunity, several should be scheduled. Pick venues which do not interfere with other events. The more of the organization's material, including visuals, that reporters use, the less a third party's material will be used.

Pools and photo opportunities may also become briefings or quasi-news conferences. The situation may require statements by officials, briefings by technical experts, demonstrations of equipment or procedures and the handing out of background materials.

While photo opportunities are meant primarily for TV crews and still photographers, radio reporters (and others) may wish to attend to see things for themselves. Give as much advance notice as possible that a pool or photo op is being organized and then post the details as to when it will begin and who will be involved at a central location. Logistics permitting, a security person should accompany public affairs/communications and media on photo opportunities.

Procedures outlined in other sections in this book for preparation of spokespeople and the conducting of briefings should be approximated as best as the physical surroundings permit. However, care must be taken to keep the event less formal than a news conference. The main objective is to show media people something they can use in their reports.

Visual audits of facilities should be undertaken to determine what photo opportunities can be offered. Pre-planning should involve testing whether successful photo opportunities can be offered on short notice. Their events should be informative (i.e. how things work, a new process) rather than entertaining or diversionary.

Reporter pools are a way for three or four reporters from representative news organizations to share limited space on an aircraft, boat or in confined quarters. They then share their stories and pictures with the reporters who could not attend. A photo opportunity allows TV and print reporters to take picture of a news event in order to compile their stories.

Before a reporter pool is formed, you'll need to alert the media and perhaps enlist their help in selecting candidates to form the pool. When a photo opportunity is scheduled, a notice should go up with all the details, so any journalists who want to attend, can (See Appendix 3, Figure 3.13).

Media Work Centre

If your organization is subject to media attention lasting several hours or perhaps even days, during which you intend to hold regular news conferences, briefings and other news-related events you should establish a separate media work centre.

This will allow newspeople to meet the needs of their individual outlets. Reporters will use it to write their reports, video-editors to view and package their visual material and others may use it to research or rest between deadlines.

Ideally this room should be different from, but close to, the news conference room, although newspeople can adapt to almost any conditions if they have to.

Signs should indicate where the media are to go, and if necessary, a map should be handed out to reporters to direct them to the proper waiting area. The media may be directed to a room off-site, perhaps in a hotel if the situation makes using organization facilities inappropriate.

Television equipment takes up an enormous amount of room. Facilities should be large and secure.

Although some small media outlets do not issue credentials to reporters, most news organizations do provide some form of identification. Such credentials should be checked and a record of the reporters maintained. A media contact form should be filled out by personnel staffing a table outside the door of the media room. When reporters are travelling to a remote location, the local hotel phone number or cell phone number for reporters should also be recorded.

Ideally, and during a prolonged stay, the Media Work Centre should contain as many reasonable amenities as possible to allow reporters to do their jobs. The single most important consideration is ample desk space, closely followed by ease of communications (phones etc.) and access to electric power (See Appendix 3, Figure 3.18).

However difficult it may be for you to accept, the fact remains your news story will be only one of dozens of stories that day. People in the news business have an insatiable appetite for knowing what is going on elsewhere and worry whether they are missing something.

If you are going to have newspeople hanging around for any length of time, try to meet that need. TV sets capable of receiving both local and national news channels should be provided, along with a notice board or table holding the latest news agency wire copy.

A courier and messenger service may also be necessary, depending on the location.

If you decide that refreshments are needed, they should be kept simple (i.e. sandwiches, water, coffee and fruit juice).

You may ask why you should go to so much trouble to look after the needs of a bunch of people you don't know and, with luck, will never meet again. It certainly won't guarantee you favourable coverage. So why do it?

As strange as it seems, reporters dislike those who openly try to influence their coverage, but respect people who make it easier for them to do their jobs the way they want to do them. Thus a properly run, temporary media centre that allows reporters to work efficiently will enhance their respect for the organization responsible.

Properly run, news conference rooms, media work centres, photo opportunities and other facilities and procedures for journalists also tells them you are competent. One of the few ways a reporter can judge you and your organization is by how you manage information. They may have trouble deciding whether you make good widgets, but they'll have little difficulty seeing that you can or can't issue a press release on time or equip a media centre.

Reporters' stories will reflect their observations.

Your abilities in setting up a functioning media work centre becomes a metaphor for your ability to run your organization well. You don't want reporters walking away from your news conference muttering, "These guys can't even get the photocopier working."

And don't forget, having a representative group of newspeople handy and happy can also work to your advantage. If the public affairs or other staff you have assigned to the media centre keep their eyes and ears open you should get some valuable feed-back on how the overall situation is developing. If they tell you your messages are not resonating despite the best efforts of your spokesperson, you will know something has to change.

Temporary Public Affairs Room

In the event an organization decides to hold a news conference "off-site" or at a location far removed from its operating base, it will be advisable to set up a temporary office for public affairs/communications personnel adjoining or close to the news conference room (See next page). This becomes twice as important if a media work centre is also established. For the duration of the event, this room inevitably becomes the hub of an organization's public affairs activities. Storage space is usually underestimated.

The room needs to be set up quickly and run smoothly. Because of the "make-do" surroundings and pressures of working under time constraints, it can quickly become a very messy and confusing environment.

Standard operating procedures will lessen confusion and increase efficiency. This consists of breaking down the organizational and operational requirements into separate tasks that can be printed out in easy-to-understand terms with simple, easy-to-follow diagrams.

The most important consideration here is efficient and secure communication with those in the organization responsible for coordinating its strategy and delivering its messages. Reporters know that a temporary office in a hotel room or tent in a field is not as secure as the one at headquarters. They're experts at thinking up excuses to gain admission and wander around looking for anything that will give them an edge over their competitors.

If the room is in operation for an extended period of time you will want to rotate the people working there. So the second most important consideration is continuity-they all need to know what has gone on during the previous shift or the few days prior to their arrival

Six hour shifts are ideal for those staffing the office. Relief staff should rotate in on a "staggered" basis so only one or two new staff join at one time. Shifts must overlap by a minimum of 15 minutes to allow for a full orientation.

Meetings should be kept to a minimum. Rotating staff can be brought up to date with status boards, by "reading into" the latest written material such as news releases and the momentary calling for silence in the room to yell announcements of new developments.

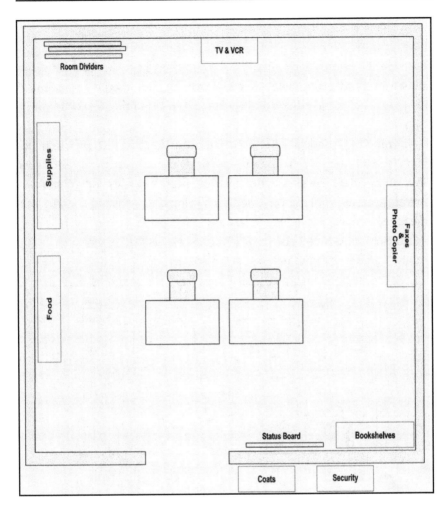

Room dividers can be used to create a privacy or rest area with one or two chairs. If the situation requires you to issue photo identification cards to reporters, room dividers can also be used to set aside an area for this.

By keeping chairs to a minimum you can cut down on the number of hangers on and uninvited visitors to this busy work room. Depending on distances involved, it may also be necessary to set up a public affairs desk in or outside the media work centre or news conference room.

It may seem like a lot of detail, but if you decide how you want to set up your media work centre now, you can just fax a diagram and list of supplies to a hotel when the need arises.

Public Affairs Desk

Each public affairs desk should be configured in a similar manner as shown in the diagram below. Newly arriving staff should feel comfortable with the surroundings and not have to search for assets or information.

Three ring binders with divider tabs by day must be kept to maintain a record of all public data issued or dealt with by the organization. The appropriate desks should have all press releases, opening statements to news conferences, media clippings or transcripts and statements by spokespeople logged in these binders.

If time and travel are considerations, hotels can be asked to set up rooms and desks in the manner described.

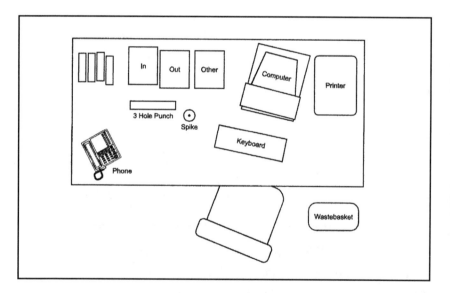

Pre-Event Checklist

> Contact public affairs/communications or an outside company for guidance on local conditions (special needs, characteristics, expectations)

> Assemble or identify locations of on- and off-site assets including rooms

> Identify and train people to assist

> Make an inventory of staff skills and outline sources of skills/assets

Checklist for Beginning of Shift

> Check all status boards for new information
> Locate the person you are relieving and obtain note or briefing
> Read into three-ring binder and ask questions as needed
> Identify deadlines or goals during your shift
> Familiarize yourself with issue and media analysis
> View, listen and read media reports

Checklist For End of Shift

> Leave "to do" or "heads up" list for incoming shift. Conduct five-minute briefings with the morning shift
> Ensure that three ring binder is up to date
> Clean desk
> Ensure contents of wastebasket are shredded if possible
> Check all status boards to ensure they are up to date with your data
> Remove personal belongings
> Log out with senior person
> Leave premises as soon as possible
> Do not reveal information while socializing off site
> View, listen and read media reports
> Do not leave draft versions of material anywhere other than in shredder

You will need supplies to run a public affairs room during an event. Thinking about these lists now can save you precious time during an event. Location, duration and complexity of the situation will determine the exact mix of assets required (See Appendix 3, Figures 3.15 and 3.16).

The Technology Trap

Hollywood story editors have filing cases filled with scripts detailing the horrors that are likely to be visited upon us when somebody – either mother nature or a fiendishly clever terrorist – throws a spanner into the delicate workings of our communications-dependent society.

It is one thing to be prepared for the media on your home turf (or head office or plant), quite another to be as well prepared off-site.

Because reporters, by definition, work off-site, they are usually able to cope when the power fails and the lights go out. If you are running a temporary public affairs room or media work centre that is unable to cope with the unexpected, your entire organizational reputation is at risk.

That's why this book has detailed lists of equipment for such temporary facilities. They allow you to make use of anyone who's available to get these rooms up and running quickly.

But just as we recommend you review and update your SOCKOs on a regular basis, so should you review these lists.

The rate of evolution in electronics and telecommunications is staggering. Twenty five years ago reporters were still carrying portable manual typewriters. Within 10 years they all had laptop computers and cell phones. These days everything is wireless and digital and able to run off battery power.

But don't get caught in the technology trap: batteries can let you down. If you want to plan for emergencies make sure you have enough chargers and spare batteries for your laptops, cell phones and pagers. Bear in mind that if conditions are so bad that you lose all power, the chargers will be useless! And then there are the printers, copiers etc.

This particular problem will be eased as soon as longer-life batteries are available. An alternative solution, however, is to make sure your temporary work facilities are also hooked up to a portable generator capable of supplying all your power needs for at least 48 hours.

I found out that we can live without technology in my work with international diplomats and disaster relief workers. They often get off a plane and start working in an area that's lost power and I had to help them do their jobs regardless. It's amazing what you can get done with drug store batteries and some ingenuity. But, without a strategy, we're all lost without modern conveniences.

Media Contacts

Records must be kept of all contacts with reporters. This is especially true when you know reporters will be covering a developing or ongoing story. Local office, site locations (hotel, rental office etc.) as well as head office interactions with reporters must be recorded. There's not much point in only knowing the Toronto address and phone number of a broadcast network when their local reporter is hounding you at the site of your incident in Alberta.

During normal business times, records must also be kept of all media inquiries and contacts (See Appendix 3, Figure 3.17). It's more difficult to manage a media relations problem when there's no accurate record of who called, why, when and what was said. Public affairs may not have to approve every interaction with the media, but should know of all media inquiries, or at least receive a briefing after the fact.

An added dimension to these forms which follow can be a place for notes on both the questions asked and answers given. Media interest in a topic can be tracked by season of the year, type of media outlet (radio, TV, print) or other criteria.

Another useful purpose: the forms can serve is to give guidance to staff who are not designated spokespeople, but may speak to reporters in chance encounters over the phone. A written company policy on dealing with the press should be widely circulated. This policy should include some rudimentary advice — of the kind found elsewhere in this book. Potential spokespeople must understand the distinction between information which is factual and readily available about the company versus information which breaks new ground, new policy or about which there may be controversy.

The former is quite safe to give out, while the latter is clearly not.

Use of Employee Skills

Most organizations pay lip service to the concept of their employees being their most valuable asset, without ever really finding out just how valuable. The media relations function is one area were this can prove to be true.

Reporters may want to speak to a worker who helped make the product or trains customers to use it. There are countless ways you can use your employees as effective spokespeople. Reporters like tours of plants and will encounter your employees along the way.

Your employees are your ambassadors whether you like it or not.

You might as well find out what skills they have and augment those with training so you have more resources at your disposal.

How you use your employees will depend on the situation and your resourcefulness (See Appendix 3, Figure 3.14). This form will help you evaluate the raw skills you have and the training needed to augment those skills.

Chapter 8   When Things Go Wrong

Setting the Record Straight

Many people get upset when their contact with or exposure in the media doesn't turn out the way they expect. This is due partly to ignorance about the media and its motives and partly to a widespread resentment of its apparent power and influence.

The solution isn't to ignore it and hope it will go away. It won't. It is far better to know something about the media you have to deal with and to have reporters know something about you. Become engaged in the process of shaping your own public image.

The most common complaint of people who have dealings with journalists is, "I was misquoted." In the vast majority of cases, however, they weren't misquoted but their words weren't used the way they expected. The complaint then becomes: "That's not what I meant to say. My words were taken out of context."

With few exceptions, reporters and their editors are not part of the stories they cover. Your context is not necessarily their context. It's their story and they control its shape, tone, texture — and context.

This isn't to suggest that reporters don't get things wrong. Your first line of defence is to make sure that what the reporter hears and records is exactly what you meant to say. This is where SOCKOs come into play.

If, in spite of your best efforts, the reporter gets it wrong and you feel strongly enough about it to want to see the error corrected there are a number of things you can do. There's no reason for anyone to feel like a helpless victim.

In the case of a factual error such as an incorrect identification or the omission of a word that completely alters the meaning of a quote, a phone call to the reporter or editor involved is usually all that's needed to see or hear a correction. But make sure your call is timely. Don't fret and fume for a week before calling. And try not to scream at the reporter before he or she has an opportunity to learn how important it is to print or broadcast a correction.

There are several different ways to set the record straight, and you must take the time to consider which one is right for the situation you are in. You must also consider which technique to use first, keeping in mind you may want a back up position should your first effort fail. You can't first threaten to sue a reporter, and then ask to have a friendly lunch. But you can have lunch first and if all else fails, consider a law suit. What follows is some advice on how to start off with a phone call or letter to the editor, and then perhaps use an op-ed article or meeting with the editorial board. The final strategy is a libel chill letter and lawsuit, which should be exercised only as a last resort.

Phone Call
> Be timely, don't delay
> Be polite
> Be firm
> Be reasonable about the prominence given to the correction (don't demand it be given a headline on the front page)

Cases where you disagree with the reporter's conclusions or feel their articles are slanted or otherwise misleading, are more complicated. News outlets won't issue a correction if there's no error in fact. But you still have options.

Call the editor or someone else in a position of authority and discuss your concerns. See if you can get a commitment to print a letter to the editor. Some broadcast organizations also air letters from viewers and listeners.

While it is your letter, it is not your newspaper or program. To make it stand out for the people who must sift through hundreds of letters everyday use the same techniques as you would in writing a media release. Use short, sharp sentences and get to the point. Make sure you have your facts right.

Try to confine your letter to the most important point you want to make. A laundry list of perceived "errors" in the story and the short-comings of the news organization and its staff may well be spiked and forgotten about. Make your point as forcefully as you can — but don't go too far. You may think the faulty story is irresponsible and that you have a right to berate and belittle your critics. But news organizations likely know more than you about the laws of libel and defamation and they won't use your letter if they think it will pose a problem.

Letter to the Editor
> Be timely, don't delay
> Be brief, stick to one or two key points
> Be logical and reasonable
> Avoid personal attacks and sweeping generalizations
> Thank them for the coverage briefly and express your view
> Avoid negatives at all cost
> Don't repeat the offense, accusation or negative

If you feel strongly that the issues raised in the original article or item cannot be dealt with adequately in a short letter, and if you think there's enough public interest in the matter, then you can submit your own article for the Opinion Section. This is the part set aside for commentary, analysis and opinion and in newspapers it is often found on the page opposite the editorials, hence the term "Op-Ed."

Anyone can submit an op-ed piece on just about any topic. An op-ed piece can help change opinion, refute charges, establish a public dialogue or make a point that no one else has made.

While articles for the op-ed page can be longer than a letter you still have to be careful to cut out all but the most important ideas you want to convey. The average length is 750 words. That may seem a lot — until you actually start to write. It's a good idea to check with the newspaper or news organization you hope will run your article to find out their rules and conditions for accepting such material.

Editors like to see strong opinions expressed but as in the case with letters, avoid laundry lists of complaints and personal attacks. This can be a platform to educate, entertain, explore new ideas or urge community action on any number of issues. It can also help establish the individual or organization as a knowledgeable source of information and reasoned opinion in certain areas. This is an opportunity worth exploring for organizations whose activities may give them public visibility.

If you do manage to "connect" with the local op-ed page in this way, you may find yourself being asked from time to time to contribute an article about or related to your particular field. But be warned: the more timely the article, the less time you will have to prepare it. Sometimes you will have only 4 or 5 hours in which to write and before you know it, you'll find yourself under the same sort of limitations that confront professional journalists every day!

Op-Ed Page Articles
> Be informative and reasoned
> Be opinionated
> Avoid personal attacks
> Claim the high ground
> Get the facts on your side
> Cite third parties to bolster your position

Letters to the editor and op-ed articles may also provide you with an opportunity to suggest a meeting with the organization's editorial board.

There are variations among newspapers, but most have a small number of senior journalists who function as an editorial board. It is their job to set the editorial policy of the newspaper and then designate one member to write the editorial expressing the position they've decided the newspaper should take. Typically a newspaper may have one long and two shorter editorials in a given day. Some news days lend themselves to two longer pieces and one short one. On occasion, editorials may be humorous or even frivolous, but most newspapers take this work very seriously.

Most editorial boards have a spirited discussion about current events or items of particular interest to them at a similar time each day. During this discussion, the board will arrive at a position and assign one of its members to write the editorial. This person then conducts research, talks with contacts and drafts the editorial. Other members may be working on other long or short editorials at the same time. The writer may show these drafts to a colleague voluntarily for input or as a mandatory procedure to those in the chain of command until the editorial appears in the newspaper. A good, fast, experienced member of an editorial board may write three or four longer and several shorter editorials each week.

Variations on this procedure involve issues of ownership and the talents of the board members. Newspaper owners may regularly play an active role in the editorial stance of the newspaper, or merely hire like-minded staff and let them do their jobs. Publishers may become similarly involved.

From time to time, however, editorial boards also meet with political, economic, business and community leaders to discuss specific interests and concerns. When that happens, reporters who may cover that specific topic — the environmental, medicine, technology or urban affairs — will be invited to attend to gain additional background in those fields and sometimes to prepare a news item based on the meeting.

Part of your strategy may be to interest the editorial board in your position on a current issue or one that will have an impact on public policy. You can request a meeting with the board. There's no guarantee they'll meet you, but if you show why your position is important for them to understand and write about, you may have a good chance.

Media relations practitioners often fail to appreciate the value of meeting with editorial boards. In fact, such encounters are as much about building relationships as they are about dispensing news. Properly handled, they can be immensely beneficial in setting the framework and context for an issue or problem in which you or your organization may be involved.

It's important that both sides have realistic expectations of the meeting and are properly prepared. The Board doesn't want to waste time asking questions the visitors can't answer and the visitors don't want to feel as if they're on the griddle. It helps if the visitors have something new to say, or can cast a current issue in a new light.

Editorial board visits work best when they anticipate an issue rather than react to it. Waiting until a negative editorial appears about your organization shows lack of planning and awareness of issues.

Treat the editorial board as you would any small group of busy people with whom you have a meeting and from whom you want something. Be clear and quick. Get to the point. Thank them for taking the time to hear you out. Be prepared to answer questions. Use visual aids, but keep it simple and on topic. Above all, remember why you are there. If necessary, ask for support or a change in the newspaper's editorial stand. You may not get it, but the request will certainly underscore your seriousness.

Meeting with Editorial Boards
> Be ahead of the issues
> Be prepared and ensure the board is aware of your role
> Be a positive news maker

These days, several major news publications have an office of "ombudsman," or reader's representative. This person investigates complaints made by the public against the paper and can recommend corrective action if that is warranted.

A number of locations also have Press Councils, or similar bodies, where members of the public can take their complaints if they feel they are not being dealt with properly by the newspaper involved. These bodies sift the evidence and render a verdict on the complaint which is duly reported by the media.

The Libel Chill Letter

However, all of the approaches outlined above take time and you may feel the published article or broadcast item is so wrong that you need to act immediately. You and your lawyer may decide there are grounds to launch legal proceedings — but that will also take time. To reduce the chances of the same errors and misconceptions being repeated you should consider a different sort of letter — a warning letter — to the reporter involved, with copies to the editor and the news outlet's lawyer.

The key elements of this letter are:
1) Acknowledgement of the reporter's interest
2) A recognition of the right of journalists to do investigative stories
3) An offer of several spokespeople to be interviewed to deal with the issues raised
4) A suggestion of several story lines of public interest other than the one the journalist is pursuing, along with background material to support this contention
5) A reference to accepted journalistic ethics regarding news gathering and the need for balance and fairness in reporting
6) A warning that dissemination of unproven information and allegations will not be tolerated and may be actionable

A sample letter follows:

Dear Ms. Journalist:

Thank you for your enquiry about the activities of the XYZ Corporation. We can understand why you would be interested in us and our activities.

We have several spokespeople you may want to interview: our CEO, our CFO, our Public Affairs Manager and our Plant Manager can all be available to you, depending on the ultimate focus of your story.

I'd like to point out that we are a leader in our field. We have several patented operations and products. We outperform our nearest competitor in a number of ways. We have an excellent environmental record and enlightened human resources policies. Attached is some background material, media clippings, our in-house newspaper and fact sheets on a number of our innovative procedures and policies.

We know you will benefit from doing more research about XYZ Corporation. We'd like you to go on a plant tour after you've read the attached. In that way you can put your interest in our activities in a proper context. You will be able to present to your readers a more accurate and complete picture of our Corporation.

I'd also like to point out that we are in compliance with all federal and local environmental regulations, and, in fact, do better than many laws require. Any suggestion, as I think you made in your questioning to me, that we are not in compliance is both inaccurate and may even be actionable.

To reiterate though, we're pleased you're interested in us. We want to help you do your story. Let us know what other information or spokespeople we can provide and we will work with to ensure an accurate, complete and balanced story.

Yours truly,

Jane Bloggs
Vice President, Corporate Communications
cc: Corporate Counsel; Editor

The reason you copy corporate counsel and the editor (section editor, producer, executive producer or other appropriate manager above the journalist) is that they are much more conservative than the journalist. Often lawyers and editors simply ask reporters if they "really need paragraph three." That's often the difference between a story you can live with and one you'd rather not have to see or hear.

Dark Websites

An Internet website can be a useful communications tool — not a stand-alone strategy. Technology is no substitute for human communication. These days nearly every organization has one, but a website is only a repository of information, rather like a filing cabinet. Those seeking information have to know where the cabinet is located, which draw to open and which file to search in.

However, a properly organized site can be of immense value in keeping stakeholders informed of an organization's purpose, activities, history, policies, products and goals. Reporters, researchers and producers will often search an organization's site for relevant information before contacting the organization itself to follow up on a story or issue of interest.

One aspect worth exploring is the establishment of a "dark" site or page, that is only "lit up" or activated when an organization decides the information it contains should be made available readily and speedily. An example might be an airline's safety record. No matter how good, this is not something airlines like to talk about and statistics on accidents are not usually made available except in response to questions.

But if the company experiences a mishap, its record is immediately relevant. A dark site containing this information — together with emergency telephone numbers and other relevant details — can be prepared and held in reserve until required. Then the dark site can be activated and the information is available to everybody.

This kind of preparation can only enhance an organization's reputation for professional competence and respect for its stakeholders, including the media and public.

CONCLUSION

If there is any conclusion to reach in a subject as vast as media relations, it may be that the discipline is a lot of work. Whether it's called communications, public affairs or by any other name, it is a labour intensive business. It concerns people, and people are as varied in their intellectual and emotional needs as they are in their physical appearance. Their needs and the needs of their organizations change within short periods of time.

With that in mind, my overall advice is two-fold: roll up your sleeves and get going with your media relations strategy, and when you're done, start all over again. I say this because just as you are making inroads and having a bit of success, that reporter who covered your issue so well will move out of town, the radio station will change from all news to an all music format and the magazine will stop taking opinion columns from you or anyone else. There will always be a certain capriciousness to such a personality driven enterprise as the media.

However, if you do use some of the tools and suggestions in this book, you will have a little more success than if you don't employ such a systematic approach. Success can be both personal and organizational. The personal success is the sense of satisfaction you can get out of seeing your items in print or on TV and radio newscasts. It can also be the fun of dealing with reporters who are eclectic and interesting people. Most of the successful media relations practitioners I know have a lot more fun than the average person in their organizations. Senior management is usually afraid of the press and grateful that someone in the communications shop is looking after reporters. If you're good at this, you can expect access to the executive suite, raises and promotions.

Organizational success can have several faces, too. It can be publicity and promotion for products or causes. This can include philanthropic efforts that can make your community a better place in which to live, work, play and learn. Success can also involve lessening dangerous situations by enhancing the organization's reputation or shortening the life of a bad news story.

There's a final exciting notion about media relations I'd like to share.

When an organization decides it must take action or change culture, very few executives can begin to help quickly. Financial audits or new controls take time. Legal action requires research and can only proceed as quickly as the courts will allow. Hiring and training from the HR department needs months to allow for placing ads, interviewing, giving notice and scheduling. New knowledge systems are dependent on the buying of computers, software and the commissioning of training. But the communications department can start making a difference in one hour. That's how long it takes to write and issue a news release, call a reporter, rehearse for an interview, plan an event, or put together a press kit. Fellow executives have to take notice of that kind of power — and once you have some of the tools this book describes in place, you can share that power in your next executive meeting.

Stay safe and have fun!

APPENDIX 1   Sample SOCKOs

What follows are some example s of SOCKOs on contentious issues from the oil industry. We all have opinions on gas prices and the environmental effects of oil industry activities. These SOCKOs show how a spokesperson can discuss these contentious issues with some positive outcome. A note of caution though: without practice and rehearsal, these are only words on a page. They must become the basis for the performance art of speaking to be convincing. A good spokesperson needs tough questions from staff as a tune up, video and audio taping for review and great research to ensure the SOCKOs are on topic and accurate.

Issue: *Tanker Safety*

SOCKO: In our ninety year history of marine operations, we have not suffered a major oil spill from a company-owned ship.

Background:

We manage marine operations in all major waterways and are engaged in the transportation of crude oil, refined petroleum products and, to a smaller extent, petrochemicals.

We have a long and honourable record of environmental responsibility. We are committed to protecting the environment and to safeguarding the health and safety of employees, and the general public.

We fully accept our duty to ensure that the hazards associated with our operations are identified, assessed and appropriately managed to minimize risks and prevent accidents.

If an accident does occur, we provide an effective and timely response in order to protect public health, employees, wildlife and the environment.

We maintain the capability to provide a rapid response to all spills, and we are prepared to escalate our response as appropriate.

The vast majority of oil spills in our waters — in fact 99.7% of them — are expected to be less than 1000 barrels.

Over the next three years we will invest about $8-10 million dollars to improve our initial response capability at our key marine terminals and spill cooperatives.

We have taken initiatives to improve safety on tankers by carrying two pilots, moderating speed and having a tug escort where appropriate.

We have taken special preventative measures: ensuring that all foreign-flag tankers we use are well-suited for their intended trade, are operated by responsible owners and have good safety and pollution avoidance records. On docking, they are attended by a contracted pollution prevention inspector who monitors, inspects and reports on the vessel's condition and performance.

We are committed to working with industry and governments to develop a response plan for all spill scenarios, including contingency plans with large catastrophic spills that would utilize both national and international resources.

Issue: *Gasoline Pricing*

SOCKO: Many studies including major government enquiries have shown that the oil industry is highly competitive and gas prices in Canada are based on dynamic market forces.

Background:

The distribution distances from refinery to gas pump is shorter in the US. Larger markets resulting in greater economy of scale allows lower gas prices in the US.

The service station prices for full service in Canada are sometimes cheaper than in the US.

The American preference for cash sales and self service accounts for some gasoline price reduction.

Over 40% of the current selling price of gasoline is tax.

In the United States, taxes on a litre of gasoline account for only about 10 cents of the pump price. Other factors that contribute to lower gasoline prices in the United States are lower refining, transportation and distribution costs and a larger, more efficient retail network.

In Canada, federal and provincial taxes, on average, account for about 24 cents per litre of gasoline. In fact, one of the single biggest sources of gasoline price increase to Canadians in recent years has been governments in the form of higher taxes.

The price of gasoline and other refined petroleum products is primarily determined by the market.

Competition is intense in the retail gasoline marketplace. There has been a sharp rise in the number of regional refiners and marketers, and small independent marketers, or "private-branders." Today, the regional and independent competitors evenly split about 40% of the market. Motorists have more choices than ever before on making their gasoline purchases.

In the long term, both the gasoline retailer-who is often an independent dealer-and the refiner and marketer, must recover their costs and earn a return on their investments in order to stay in business. Retailers receive about 4 to 5 cents per litre of gasoline to cover their operating costs and earn an income and return on their investment. The refiner and marketer receives about 15 to 16 cents per litre to cover operating, distribution and marketing costs, pay income tax and provide a profit margin. According to the federal Petroleum Monitoring Agency, the profit margin for the refining/marketing sector of the Canadian petroleum industry has typically been about one cent per litre of petroleum product.

The Petroleum Monitoring Agency reports that for a 5-year period studied, the industry's average return on capital has been 4% — substantially less than an individual can earn in many risk-free bank investments.

Issue: *Global Warming/Greenhouse Effect*

SOCKO: Our company has conducted extensive research in this area and we've been able to reduce the impact our operations used to have on the environment.

Background:

We are responsible for about 2% of CO_2 emissions from fossil fuel combustion and a lesser share of the other direct greenhouse gas emissions.

The company has conducted a comprehensive examination of the potential for further energy efficiency improvements to reduce CO_2 and other combustion-related greenhouse gas emissions in its operations.

We have completed an inventory of greenhouse gas emissions resulting from our operations. It includes CO_2, methane(CH_4), nitrous oxide (N_2O) and chlorofluorocarbons (CFCs) and the indirect greenhouse gasses, namely nitrogen oxides (NO_x) and volatile organic compounds (VOCs). NO_x and VOCs are precursors of ozone (O_3), a greenhouse gas.

We believe it is technically feasible to dispose of about 3.5% of CO_2 emissions into subterranean formations at a cost of $15 to $50 per tonne of CO_2.

Alternate transportation fuels offer somewhat limited potential to reduce-and in some cases actually increase greenhouse gas emissions.

We have been a consistent leader in developing more efficient burning fuels and new combustion methodology.

Improved refining techniques and technology have dramatically reduced fuel contaminants. We have a vital stake in the development of environmental public policy and are committed to taking an active role.

There is an urgent need to reduce uncertainties and to improve understanding and awareness of both the scientific and socio-economic dimensions of the threat of climate change.

Steps can be taken now without weakening the country's ability to compete in a global trading economy.

APPENDIX 2   News / Media Terms & Definitions

(Do not use these terms in casual conversation with reporters since it will sound false.)

Actuality
Recording of a person who is part of a news story.

Air Date
The date that the story will be broadcast.

Ambient Sound
The natural sound occurring in a room or location.

Angle
The "hook" or particular emphasis of a story.

Assignment Editor
Quasi-management position in broadcast newsrooms responsible for matching reporters with stories.

B-Roll
Term used for video scenes used to supplement or to compliment the story. Can be scenes recorded during the visit to your location (cover shot), stock footage or scenes from the station's video library.

Background
Information used to add context and depth to a story.

Betacam
Broadcast quality shoulder-held camera used by TV networks and stations.

B/G (see Ambient sound)
Background sound, usually at a lower level than the voice over.

Bridging Shot
A scene or series of scenes used to cover edit points in the finished production. Also known as cover shot or B roll.

Broadcast Quality
Video picture clarity good enough for broadcast. VHS and other home-movie formats are not and used only in special circumstances.

Cans
Headphones.

Chocolate Bar
The nickname given to the small battery (NP-1) used in Betacam equipment.

Copy Editor
Supervising journalist who reviews and improves the output of news writers.

Cover Shot
Scenes relating to the story used to cover the edit point. Also known as B roll or bridging shot.

Cut Line Writer
Newspaper or magazine employee who writes the captions for pictures.

Dolly
Moving a studio camera, usually referring to a lateral move.

Double-Ender
During a double-ender, the interviewer is in the studio while the person being interviewed is in some remote location. Also known as a remote interview.

EFP
Electronic Field Production. Term used to cover video productions out-

146 / ALLAN BONNER

side a studio setting.

Fact Checker
Usually a magazine employee who calls interview subjects after the fact to ensure statistics and quotations to be used are accurate.

File Tape or Footage
Visual material recorded previously. This footage may come from the news organization's own library, an outside library or even from the company or organization that is the subject of the news story.

Framing
The composition of the scene.

Freelance
Journalist who regularly works on an item by item basis for a number of media outlets.

Intro
The opening segment of a news story, sometimes with the reporter on camera doing a stand-up. Often it is the last segment of the story to be recorded. Reporters like stand-ups in front of plants, spills and other visuals.

Lavelier Mike
A small microphone that is pinned or clipped to the shirt, blouse or tie. It is generally used during interviews and by the news anchor in the studio.

Lead
The all-important opening sentence or paragraph of a news story or media release.

Lighting Kit
Portable lights used during interior interview.

Line-up Editor

Newsroom position for a writer/editor who ensures the news stories of the day are ordered, read or "lined up" in a logical sequence. This sequence often relies on geography, themes, disciplines (economics, war, etc.) importance to large numbers of news consumers or other factors.

Live on Air

An interview broadcast live and taped for possible re-use during later broadcasts.

Live to Tape

An interview broadcast as recorded, un-edited.

MCU

Medium close-up. A camera shot, which, when referring to a shot of a person would be a head and shoulders shot from a comfortable distance. A medium close up of a building would be from a greater distance. Newscasters and reporters doing "stand up" are usually medium close ups. Closer shots are referred to as close-ups. A "60 minutes" close up is so close that it may feature the face from just under the hair line to just before the chin.

On Camera

A term used for any subject or item recorded. The reporter talking to the camera. Also known as a "stand-up."

NTSC

National Television Standards Committee. The name given to the television system used in North America and not compatible with any other. Also see PAL, SECAM.

Page Make-Up

The person responsible for ensuring a logical and aesthetically pleasing layout of news, features, columns, graphics and/or advertisements in a newspaper or magazine.

PAL

Phase Attenuation by Line. The television standard developed and used by all western European countries except France. Also see NTSC, SECAM.

Pedestal

A camera move in a TV studio. Used as a verb, the term means to move the entire camera, not just the lense up or down. "Pedestal up," or "pedestal down" are the directions used.

Phone-In

Usually by radio, now being used on television. Viewers phone questions in to the station during a live broadcast.

Photo Editor

Decision maker responsible for choosing among the output of a variety of photographers at a magazine, wire service or newspaper.

Producer

Person responsible for radio or TV programs going to air. Associate producers often do research and invite guests on shows. Field producers go to the scene of events with reporters and supervise. The term executive producers applies to the senior producer on a program, or may merely be an honorific in a small media outlet.

Production Assistant (Control Room):

Formerly called script assistants, the "P.A.,"handles a number of complicated logistics and timing elements to ensure a smooth running and ending of the program. Continuous "back times" assist the producer and on-air personnel (via the P.A./Studio) in knowing how much time is left in each item, for an ad lib or to the end of the show. The P.A. also handles some clerical work in the production unit.

Production Assistant (Studio):

Also called floor director who relays directions from the producer in control room to newscasters, interviewers and other performers in the studio. This person gives hand signals regarding time and camera positions to on-air performers in television.

Reaction Shot
Recorded after the interview, this is often a shot of the reporter listening or reacting to the interview. This is used in editing.

Re-Ask
Recorded after an interview for editing purposes. The camera is re-positioned (usually behind you and facing the reporter) to record the reporter asking the questions.

Roll-Up (Intro)
The introduction that is read by the television news anchor before the story is broadcast. It sets the scene for the audience.

Scrim
Light defusing material used on television lights to soften or reduce the intensity.

SECAM
Sequential Colour Au Memoire. Television system developed in France, modified and used by former Soviet dominated countries. Also see NTSC, PAL.

Shot Gun Mike
A speciality microphone (like a Parabolic Mike) used to record background sound effects or a voice track from a distance, so a microphone is not visible on camera. Often used at sports events to get sound from the playing area, it is also used to record in an area with high background noise.

SFX
Sound effects. Background audio, equipment or mechanical noise.

Stand-Up
A scene where the reporter makes a statement in front of the camera.

This can be used to open the story (intro) part way through the story to bring together disparate elements and to finish the story (extro or wrap). See *On Camera*.

Stringer
Journalist who regularly works on an item by item basis for a particular media outlet, often with a more formalized relationship than a freelance.

Sun Gun
A small battery powered video light attached to the top of the video camera.

Super
A term used for the name and other information electronically printed on the television screen when the news story is broadcast.

Tape Delay
Usually used by radio stations to prevent obscene statements being broadcast during live phone in programs.

Techie
Video or audio technician.

Tighten Up
This can refer to shortening audio or video material, or to a closer framing of the subject in a television.

Tilt
A camera movement up or down. Unlike a pedestal movement, a tilt only is like a tilt of the head, as opposed to standing up or sitting down while keeping the eyes looking straight forward.

TBC
Time Base Corrector. Electronic equipment is used to modify or adjust the picture quality of the video signal. The unit used to "fix it in post."

Two Shot
Two people in the scene. In an interview this arrangement can be used as a cutaway or bridging scene. Usually the scene is shot over the reporter's shoulder facing the interviewee or while recording the re-action shots: the interviewer's back to the camera.

Videographer
Combination camera operator and reporter who both takes the pictures and asks the questions.

Voice Over (V/O)
The reporter's narration usually recorded at the television studio and used with cover shots or video stock footage scenes.

Wrap
The end of an interview story. Wrap up.

White Balance
The method of electronically adjusting the video camera to current lighting conditions. Basically inside and outside light have what are called different colour temperatures. If this adjustment is not made the skin colour will appear unnatural.

Zoom
Zooming in shows more detail in a tighter frame. Zoom out shows less in a long shot.

APPENDIX 3   Charts and Worksheets

FIGURE 3.1
Communications Matrix

PERSON/GROUP	ACTIVITY	DESIRED RESULT	FREQUENCY	COST
Senior Elected Officials				
Selected Cabinet Ministers				
Mayors				
Selected Other City Officials				
Business				
Citizens Groups				
Editorial Boards				
Reports/Editors/Interviewers				
Selected Media Managers				
Selected Educators				
Selected Other Officials				
Other Boards				
Industry Associations				

FIGURE 3.2
Media Liaison Plan

MONTH	ACTIVITY	ISSUE	TARGET/AUDIENCE	DESIRED RESULT	COST	RESPONSIBLE
January						
February						
March						
April						
May						
June						
July						
August						
September						
October						
November						
December						

FIGURE 3.3

An Analysis of Newsworthiness — The Press Release/Statement

W5	TIMELINESS	PROXIMITY	NO. OF PEOPLE AFFECTED	LASTING IMPORTANCE	GEOGRAPHICAL DISPERSAL
WHO will benefit?					
WHAT is being done?					
WHEN will this happen?					
WHY now?					
HOW will it work?					

FIGURE 3.4

Media Advisory

[Headline for Event or Announcement]

1. **WHO**   Who will be there? Who are you? How the product or policy will work.

2. **WHAT**   What is the event about? What celebrities or officials will be there?

3. **WHEN**   Day, date and time.

4. **WHERE**   Detailed directions on how to get there.

5. **WHY**   Why the event is being held and what makes it newsworthy.

CONTACT: Name of contact person. Telephone number.

FIGURE 3.5

Journalistic Questions to Rehearse with Spokespeople

INFORMATION	WHO	WHEN	WHERE	WHAT/HOW MANY	WHY	HOW
Policy						
Procedure						
History						
Effects						
Hero						
Experts						
Knows More about This						
Cost						
Benefit						
Legislation/I am						
Cause of Incident						
Related Incident						
What Happened						
Witness Opinion						
Regulation						
Facts						
Documents Saved/Lost						
Anecdotes						

FIGURE 3.6

News Conference Room Checklist

Asset	Responsibility	Completed
6-8 foot tables/20-50 chairs		
2 table cloths and curtains		
6 name cards		
Podium and lectern		
1 water pitcher and glasses (no ice)		
2 risers for TV cameras		
TV lighting (contact 3rd party supplier)		
Microphones		
Pool feed system		
Stock footage on ¾" or Betacam		
VHS camera to record		
Maps/photographs/charts		
Cover (with removable plastic only)		
Visual aids (boom, shovel etc.)		
Easels/pointer		
PA system		
Conference or audio tape machine		
20 VHS tapes/20 audio cassettes		
Status boards		
4 room dividers		
Sign-in sheets		
Background materials		
Portable toilets (if needed)		
Other		

FIGURE 3.7

News Conference Activity Checklist

Activity	Responsibility	Completed
Acquire and Set Up Room		
Call and Commission Outside Resources: 1. 2. 3.		
Refreshments		
Set out Background Material		
Obtain Assets (see list)		
Check Equipment		
Operate Fax and Photocopier		
Staff Room – Greet Reporters		

FIGURE 3.8
News Conference Final Checklist

ACTIVITY	RESPONSIBILITY	COMPLETED
Complete list of media attending		
Notify press who may be absent but should attend		
Compile information/media kits for reporters		
Invite outside officials		
Check physical arrangements for news conference		
Prepare written statement or notes for the speaker		
Review news stories to date and brief spokespeople		
Give advance copies of all materials to all relevant participants and managers		
Develop anticipated questions for the speaker/expert		
Circulate among reporters before to determine interest level and/or questions		
Prepare local issues brief		
Alert and brief technical experts		
Escort spokespeople to dressing/quiet room		
Rehearse spokespeople/experts		
Alert reporters on site		
Update status boards (see "Public and Media Update" and "Information Opportunities") and visual aids		
Staff tables outside press briefing room		

FIGURE 3.9
Status Board

Information Current as of: (Date and Time)	
Location	
Persons Dead: Injured: Displaced:	
Property Destroyed: Damaged: Estimated Cost:	
Services Interrupted When: What: Where: Duration:	
Trade Figures	
Cultural Ties	
Assets Deployed	
Cause Determined 1. 2. 3.	
Other	

FIGURE 3.10
Media Update

Information Current as of: (Date and Time)	
Location	
Persons Promoted/Laid Off/Discharged Arrested/Charged/Missing Suits/Class Action	
Homes Built on Landfill Condemned Zoning/Tax Issues	
Businesses Bankruptcy/Default of Guarantee Product Recall/Discontinued Share Value	
Public Property Change of Use Condemned/State of Disrepair Sold/Leased	
Services Interrupted or Restored When What Where Duration	
Cultural Policy	
Assets Deployed	
Trade Figures	
Other	

FIGURE 3.11
Outside Resources

NEWS CONFERENCE ROOM

Location _____ Room Number (s) _____

Address _____

City _____ Province/State _____ Postal/Zip _____

Contact _____ Office Phone _____ Home _____

Cottage _____ Alternative _____ Fax _____

Key Reporters _____

Map and/or directions to Site _____

A/V EQUIPMENT/FOOD/LEGAL/PUBLIC RELATIONS/ADVERTISING/VIDEO PRODUCTION/PHOTO SERVICES

Organization _____

[Include same information as above]

FIGURE 3.12

Checklist: Reporter Pool/Photo Opportunity

ACTIVITY	RESPONSIBILITY	COMPLETED
Contact security and senior management to identify potential problems, including safety		
Identify interesting and camera-friendly locations and assets		
Scout location for safety and security concerns		
Plan itinerary		
Compile list of media attending		
Post pool/photo-op times in media work centre or other useful location		
Notify media in person or by phone at least 15 minutes before event		
Preparation of materials and/or equipment		
Obtain all needed safety gear and distribute to media as needed		
Conduct safety briefing for participants		
Have all media sign indemnification agreements when needed		
Preparation of potential spokespeople or experts		
Provide advance warning to people affected that media will be moving into the area		

FIGURE 3.13

Media Advisory for Reporter Pool/Photo Opportunity

[Headline for Event or Announcement]

1. WHO		Who will be there? Who are you? How the product or policy will work.
2. WHAT		What is the event about? What celebrities or officials will be there?
3. WHEN		Day, date and time.
4. WHERE		Detailed directions on how to get there.
5. WHY		Why the event is being held and what makes it newsworthy.
CONTACT:		Name of contact person. Telephone number.

FIGURE 3.14

Employee Inventory Skills

SKILL	PERSON	DATE CONFIRMED
Knowledge of operations, technologies, systems etc.		
Media relations/training		
Public speaking		
Knowledge of history of organization		
Languages (list)		
Other		

FIGURE 3.15

Equipment Checklist: Public Affairs Room

ASSET/ACTIVITY	RESPONSIBILITY	COMPLETED
4 desk and chair sets, 2-4 extra chairs		
Coat rack and hanger		
Room dividers		
Paper shredder and waste baskets		
Steel filing cabinet with lock		
Flip charts, status and notice boards, 3-ring binders		
Telephone, including a secure "hotline" and answering machines		
Capability for teleconferencing or speaker phones		
Cell phones/pagers for inter-staff communications		
50 carbon message pads		
3 external phone books (white and yellow pages)		
3 internal (company) directories		
Fax machine(s) with spare rolls/reams of paper		
2 photo copiers with extra toner		
Computers, modems, printers		
Extra toner cartridges, computer disks, paper		
10 cardboard filing cases		
File folders, hangers and storage boxes		
Cardboard box for chronological newspaper storage		
Professional, trade association or other directories		
2 French/English/Spanish dictionaries		
2 Thesauri		
Media and Government lists		

FIGURE 3.16

Event Checklist: Public Affairs Room

ASSET/ACTIVITY	RESPONSIBILITY	COMPLETED
Style books		
Phone lists of key media and media directories		
Fact sheets		
Photographs of spokespeople and site (8X10, black and white)		
Recent and current news releases		
Annual reports, organizational charts, site maps etc.		
Organizational letterhead, envelopes		
Capability for teleconferencing or speaker phones		
Paper clips, tape, markers, pencils, erasers etc.		
Scissors, stapler, rubber bands, white out		
4 rolls of scotch tape, duct tape, 2 rolls of masking tape, thumb tacks		
2 TVs		
2 programmable VCRs and video camera		
3 AM/FM radios with recording ability		
Tape recorder, headphones		
Audio and video cassettes		
Dubbing wires, extension cables and power bars		
Spare batteries for all electronic equipment		
Large wall clock		
20 garbage bags and 6 rolls of paper towels		
Clerical support, couriers, catering		
Provisions for emergency lighting, power etc.		
Portable toilets (if needed)		

FIGURE 3.17
Media Contacts

RADIO

Name of Reporter _____ Network/Station _____

Address _____

City _____ Province/State _____ Postal/Zip _____

Office Telephone _____ Fax _____ Additional _____

News Director _____ Main News Deadlines _____

Coverage Area _____ Estimated Priority * _____

Subject Matter _____

Summarize Questions:

    1. _____

    2. _____

    3. _____

Summarize Answers:

    1. _____

    2. _____

    3. _____

Comments:

PRINT/TELEVISION

[Include same information as above]

FIGURE 3.18

Media Work Centre: Equipment Checklist

ASSET/ACTIVITY	RESPONSIBILITY	COMPLETED
Chairs, work desks, tables		
Coat racks and hangers		
Phone line with data transmission capabilities		
Fax, photocopier and paper		
Note pads, pens and pencils		
Large wall clock		
Waste basket		
Power bars and extension cords		
VCR/TVs		
Flip chart, status boards, notice boards, information boards (update hourly)		
Visual aids		
Background material, photos etc. (update and review hourly)		
Podium, sound equipment, bullhorn		
Refreshments (review hourly)		
Courier/messenger service		
Portable toilets (if needed)		

Selected Bibliography

Ailes, Roger, *You are the Message*, Oxford University Press, Toronto, 1988.

Bohere, G., *Profession: Journalist*, International Labour Organisation, Geneva, 1984.

Bonner, W. Allan, "The Mechanics of Media Relations", Carole N. Markham, Ed., *Bout de Papier*, Vol. 6, No. 4, 1989

Bonner, W. Allan, "Off The Record: Playing the Media Game Means Playing by the Rules", *Law Times*, Vol. 4, No. 21, 1993, Paula Kulig, Managing Editor.

Bonner, W. Allan, "Off The Record: It Pays To Do Your Homework Before Talking To The Media", *Law Times*, Vol. 4, No. 29, 1993, Paula Kulig, Managing Editor

Boynton, Phil Ross, *Winning the Media Game: How to Work the Media*, Stoddart, Toronto, 1989.

Brady, John, *The Craft of Interviewing*, Random House, New York, 1976.

Broadcast News, *Style*, Broadcast News, Toronto, 1978.

Broughton, Irv, *The Art of Interviewing for Television, Radio & Film*, Tab Books, Inc., Pittsburgh, 1981.

Eliot, Deni, Ed., *Responsible Journalism*, Sage Publications, Beverly Hills, 1986.

Parkhurst, William, How To Get Publicity, Times Books, Toronto, 1985.

Pavlik, John V., *Public Relations*, Sage Publications, Beverly Hills, 1987.

Rice, Ronald E. & Atkin, Charles K., Ed., *Public Communications Campaigns*, Sage Publications, Beverly Hills, 1981.

Ries, Al & Trout, Jack, *Positioning: The Battle of Your Mind*, McGraw-Hill Ryerson, Toronto, 1981.

Rosenthal, Raymond, Ed., *McLuhan Pro & Con*, Penguin, Baltimore, 1969.

Smith, Anthony, Ed., *Newspapers and Democracy*, MIT Press, Cambridge, 1980.

Stone, Gerald, *Examining Newspapers: What Research Reveals About America's Newspapers*, Sage Publications Inc., Beverly Hills, 1987.

The Canadian Press, *Stylebook*, The Canadian Press, Toronto, 1983

The Canadian Press, *Caps and Spelling*, The Canadian Press, Toronto, 1981

Photos

One of the toughest formats is the panel discussion. Many guests feel that the object on television is to disagree with fellow panelists. You're actually best off delivering short, interesting comments. Have the audience remember your ideas, not that you disagree with someone else's ideas. Here I am in the difficult middle seat on an election panel with a pollster and columnist. To avoid swivelling my head back and forth, I try to direct most comments to the host, or just lean a little to the other guest.

Many news channels fill up the screen with lots of data. Here I am on my first book tour competing with the weather, the economy, traffic and news. In this format, you have to be especially interesting, both verbally and visually to succeed.

The middle territory is important in the side by side interview. With this business reporter, I'm leaning into the encounter and gesturing into the middle ground. Television hosts want action and passion, and so does the audience.

Whether you're seated, standing, at a desk or on a stool, a camera can always zoom in for a close up. This is a medium close up. Note how the director has his station ID, New York 1, nicely framed in the background.

In this morning talk show format the set designer has mocked-up a restaurant set. Several other people are looking on, playing the role of early morning diners. In a commercial break, I asked one who she was, but she wouldn't answer. Little things like this can throw you off, if you're not focused and practiced.

This format involves being at right angles, a good distance apart. The soft couch presents the danger of sinking in, so I have to remember to sit up and lean forward. Most hosts are just looking for an upbeat few minutes from the guest. This host was one of many to be very hospitable, including holding my book up to the camera. A guest should not arrive with a chip on his shoulder.

This TV show is set in a huge farmer's market. It's good to arrive early because the sheer size of the room can change how you hear your own voice. Note also the host's casual look. The rule is for guests to dress about a notch up from the host.

I'm often told I speak like a host, rather than like a guest. That's because I was one for years. Here, I've brought more papers to this business show than the host did.

A scrum is a Canadian term describing how several reporters may want to speak with you all at once. The term is from the game of rugby where countless players push and shove to get to the ball. To complete the metaphor, the reporters are players and the newsmaker is the ball. In England it's sometimes called 'doorstopping' because a politician emerges from a doorway to countless questions from reportors. Regardless of what you call it, the trick is to look at one reporter at a time and stay calm. The close up shot focuses on the newsmaker with only the hands and microphones of reporters showing. The crowd may look intimidating to the newsmaker, but the audience only sees you.

Here's a studio 'double-ender.' The name comes from the fact that I'm at one end looking at the lense of a camera and the host is at the other end, in a studio, interviewing a TV set with me on it. The newsmaker might be in his office or the scene of an event. Here, I've been asked to sit in the TV studio and the host is ten desks away, facing in the same direction. It ends up looking good, but listening to the host in an ear phone and staring into the lense takes concentration.

ALLAN BONNER
Ctr for Training in Risk & Crisis Mgmt.

CTV

Note how directors can edit a double ender so both the guest and host can be seen.

Allan Bonner
Int'l Crisis Management Expert

The round table and high stools constitute a popular set these days. Often the rest of the studio is either buzzing with activity or pitch black. Guests must focus on their messages and the host to do well.